To those who open their hearts and lift others up,
especially when it's tough to do.

And to my Mom, whose final gift I will always cherish—
to quiet my mind and be present with my heart.

"It's clear that not all business leadership books are created equal. **Heart First** is a one-of-a-kind book for leaders featuring smart, engaging tips, presented in an easy-to-read fashion, that helps every leader successfully lead employees through change."
    – John Groetelaars, President & CEO, Hillrom

"As we begin to emerge from these unprecedented times where radical change and uncertainty about the future remain at the forefront, there is nothing more important than authenticity, candor and compassion from leaders at every level. **Heart First** provides incredible insights that empower leaders to connect with who they are and care personally about their teams, all while challenging them to be their very best. David shares inspiring yet practical messages that illustrate true leadership. This is a must-read for leaders at every level."
    – Julie Peffer, CFO, MedeAnalytics

"In these times of unprecedented change, David has provided an inspirational yet practical guide that will allow leaders to enhance their organizations and create opportunities from challenges."
    – Keith Weidman, CEO, Form Technologies

"I've known David for more than two decades, and he's a consummate coach and consultant. In **Heart First**, he captures what he knows works for more compassionate and courageous leadership. **Heart First** comes at a time when we desperately need strong leadership to carry us through this difficult period in history. It's a must read for any leader who wants to stand out and leave a lasting legacy with their teams."
    – Perry Stuckey, SVP and CHRO, Eastman

"David Grossman is my go-to expert to help senior executives communicate with passion and clarity. In his new book, **Heart First**, Grossman explores how leaders can bring their 'best selves' into the workplace. This beautiful book takes readers on a journey from knowing yourself to caring for yourself, to sharing yourself with others in meaningful and powerful ways. As a psychologist and a performance coach, I know that Grossman's lessons are crucially important for executive effectiveness. I'll be sharing this book with my clients and referring to it myself as well."

    – Gail Golden, MBA, Ph.D., Principal, Gail Golden Consulting, and author of
      Curating Your Life: Ending the Struggle for Work-Life Balance

"**Heart First** is a phenomenal read. When the world 'paused' in the midst of a global pandemic, a variety of executives 'went to work' and redefined – and practiced – what it meant to truly lead in an altered world, frequently asking themselves, 'how does the individual employee feel?' and 'how do I best connect with my team?' The various personal examples and actionable frameworks invite readers to self-reflect and become a better leader."

    – Gérard van Spaendonck, Managing Director and Operating Partner, JLL Partners

"David Grossman's **Heart First** is both timeless and timely. The lessons, stories, and insights remind us of what great leaders through the centuries have known; lessons grounded in human relations and still too often forgotten and maybe even more rare in an age of algorithms, data, and technology-centric business operations. Written during a pandemic, with our country economically and politically reeling, the knowledge and teachings in **Heart First** have never been more important or urgent."

    – Paul LeBlanc, President of Southern New Hampshire University

"As an avid reader and life-long learner, I thoroughly devoured every page of **Heart First**. Given David's rich business background, I was not at all surprised to discover and appreciate this book's best practices on what makes individuals and organizations succeed in today's challenging business environment. I especially appreciated David's thoughts on the importance of authenticity, communication, and empathy, since they are in direct alignment with my thoughts, beliefs, and core values. I know you will enjoy reading this entertaining and educational book as much as I did."
– Kevin Sheridan, Keynote Speaker & New York Times Best Selling Author

"David understands how busy his readers are, especially during the pandemic. His book is a polished gem that you can appreciate one facet at a time in manageable chunks of time. His book includes personal insights shared by business leaders, professional communicators and David himself that take only a few minutes to read, but that leave you thinking for a few minutes more. And just as you're trying to figure out how to apply those insights to your own leadership style, David shares to the point short lists of things we can start applying right now, based on his years of consulting with client leaders and his own role as leader of The Grossman Group. He both moves our hearts and gives us the tools to put our hearts into our communications."
– Angela Sinickas, CEO, Sinickas Communications, Inc.

*"David has developed a master playbook to address common situations and conflicts in our rapidly changing, highly challenging work environment. This book helps readers know how to anticipate challenges and then resolve them with authenticity and courage. **Heart First** is a must read for anyone who calls themselves a leader."*
  – Jim Karas, #1 New York Times bestselling author and entrepreneur

*"**Heart First** offers valuable insights to help organizational leaders navigate the diverse personal and professional challenges of leading with empathy, courage and clarity during turbulent times in order to have more empowering, equitable, just and inclusive impact."*
  – Daniel B. Frank, Ph.D., Principal, Francis W. Parker School

*"Most business leaders are taught to separate their emotions from work but the most successful leaders know how to tap into their emotions to connect and inspire associates. David Grossman shows readers how to be their best by doing just that. Inspired and inspiring— that is what **Heart First** is for leaders."*
  – Farah Speer, Senior Vice President, Corporate Communications, Novartis Gene Therapies

*"**Heart First** is loaded with powerful stories and valuable tips for all leaders and those aspiring to become authentic leaders. From the personal stories and actionable advice to the elegant illustrations and graphics, everything in this book is authentic and beautifully told."*
  – Ron Culp, Professional Director, Public Relations & Advertising Program, DePaul University

ACCLAIM FOR HEART FIRST

*"In his book **Heart First**, David manages to get to the core of good communication skills, particularly in times of change and during challenges, when we are all likely to need them. Physicians and academic leaders are frequently placed in positions of leadership without adequate training in self-awareness, the lack of which may lead to being inauthentic. David correctly points to knowing oneself first before acting to be our best self and presenting ourselves as authentic leaders. David's book and expert advice within will ensure that leaders reach heights of success so that they can lead the healthcare systems of the future."*

– Bhagwan Satiani MD, MBA, FACHE, FACS, Professor of Surgery Emeritus, The Ohio State University College of Medicine

"The year 2020 brought us many challenges. David does a beautiful job capturing real-life lessons learned from the frontlines of pandemic and social change related communications."

– Cy Wakeman, New York Times Bestselling author of No Ego

*"David Grossman's unbridled passion for helping leaders become the very best versions of themselves is manifest in **Heart First**! His simple yet profound message about the power of kindness, authenticity and caring will inform…and dare I say, transform…even the most skeptical of leaders. In **Heart First**, David opens his own heart in ways that challenge, encourage and edify!"*

– Jeff Outten, Chief Change Officer, Dixon Hughes Goodman LLP

"Coming through one of the most challenging years in our company's 90+ year history, David has captured the essence of what it takes to lead and succeed through the most demanding of circumstances. In **Heart First**, he shares lessons that focus on authentic leadership at its very core, which are critical as we lead our global business through a global pandemic, and more meaningfully, beyond it."
– Lucia Stetson, Chief of Staff and Director of PMO, Form Technologies

"David Grossman is a storyteller. I first partnered with David years ago because I wanted help becoming a better communicator and leader of people. One of the many pieces of wisdom he shared was, 'Tell more stories.' I wasn't used to being vulnerable with my employees, but I soon realized it's truly through stories that people connect with one another and internalize concepts and feelings, which was critical to my success as a leader.

In **Heart First**, David does a brilliant job of bringing personal, heartfelt stories together from leaders with diverse backgrounds to capture some of the best leadership lessons learned through the pandemic and social unrest of 2020. If you want to lead effectively through significant crisis or change, consider **Heart First** your playbook to do it right."
– John Greisch, Chairman Of The Board, Viant Medical

ISBN: 978-1-63901-202-2

Library of Congress Control Number: 2021910458

Printed in the United States of America.
This book is printed on acid-free paper.

Images provided by Shutterstock.com, all rights reserved.

HEART F1RST

LASTING LEADER LESSONS
FROM A YEAR THAT CHANGED EVERYTHING

by **DAVID GROSSMAN** ABC, APR, Fellow PRSA

LEADERS TOUCH A HEART BEFORE THEY ASK FOR A HAND

JOHN C. MAXWELL

EVERYONE
HAS A STORY

As a black woman in corporate America, I've had a bit of a double persona for many years—one person in the office and another at home. I wanted to be recognized as a professional, not as a black woman, and so there were parts of my life and story that I just tucked away, never to be shared inside a business meeting of any kind.

THAT WORKED FOR DECADES ... UNTIL IT DIDN'T

What I've realized over time is that the most important part of leading people is connecting with them in an authentic way, not just through small talk. For me, that kind of connection is built through understanding someone else's journey and someone else's story. It's also about just recognizing the simple fact that everyone has a story, a story that helps define who they are, what they hope to accomplish, and what truly matters to them when it comes to work and life.

ALISA MCGOWAN

EXECUTIVE VICE PRESIDENT AND
CHIEF HUMAN RESOURCES OFFICER, TECOMET

RECOGNIZING MY OWN STORY

As part of that, I went through a "learning lab" training, which included a facilitated conversation for black women. Our facilitator wanted us to talk about what it meant to be a black woman in corporate America. When she first asked that question, my black colleagues and I just nervously laughed. Then we looked at each other with the same question mark on our faces—I knew we were all asking, "Are you kidding me? Where do we even start....?"

By the end of that day, we began to share what it felt like candidly, with vulnerable stories that took courage to tell. The common theme was that working as a black woman leader felt like an exercise in leaving part of yourself outside the corporate doors. We all felt we had become "professionals" with masks on, for fear of not being accepted and out of a desire to be invisible.

I'm grateful that through that experience, I started to realize that I was sacrificing who I was to be accepted, and it just didn't feel good anymore. It definitely didn't feel authentic. The experience forced me to ask myself this: If I'm not living an authentic life, how can I ever be true and real to other people?

BECOMING AN AUTHENTIC LEADER

From there, I decided to start living a more authentic life. My first target was my hair. I grew up in the 80s and 90s, thinking that to be accepted in the boardroom, you had to have straight hair. That meant having plenty of relaxer on hand so my hair didn't curl up, and looked perfectly straight.

The first step in my journey to authenticity was my decision to walk into Rockwell Automation one Monday morning as a new woman. Leading up to the day, I grew out my hair, then cut it really short so it was naturally curly. It was such a simple thing, but it felt so bold to me. I couldn't believe how free I felt as I walked down the corridors. Naturally, I didn't know what to expect that morning, but two things happened that had an immediate impact on me.

"PROFESSIONALS WITH MASKS"

"

I COULDN'T BELIEVE HOW
FREE I FELT "

As I walked down the hall to see my boss, the vice president of human resources, I heard her enthusiastically wave me in. She had been with me during the learning lab training and knew how bothered I was by that conversation. She looked at me for a moment, then said simply: "You have just proven something to me; people are most beautiful the way they naturally are."

That really, really got me. And just as I was taking that in, I walked past another office and down the corridor to find another leader flagging me down, suggesting I step in. He, too, had been at the same training and knew my hair story. He smiled and just said, "You look great."

THE POWER BEHIND FINDING YOUR OWN VOICE

I was scared to death of what people would think and yet I just made the decision to step out there and do what I felt was right, and it's been the most impactful experience. Since then, that's how I've tried to lead, to be courageous, transparent, authentic, and try to understand other people's stories. It's been a heck of a journey, but I think I'm a better leader for it.

I do wish it hadn't taken me so long to recognize this simple learning in my own life. It's not that I wasn't a good listener or didn't have quality conversations with colleagues and fellow leaders. But I held back too much, stopping short of truly getting to know people. And I hadn't taken the critical step to start with myself. It's a straight-forward learning, but a profound one, especially in these times of racial unrest and amid so many questions about how to build a better culture at work.

I see it as coming down to this: Everyone has a story and the simple task of sharing it—and having the presence of mind as the listener to take it in—is one of the most important lessons for leaders today. That lesson is critical for leaders who want to build the kind of workplace that is not only diverse, but inclusive of diverse thought, and welcoming. This is the kind of workplace I want for Tecomet, where people are so comfortable and accepted that they are excited to come to work every day.

LEADING WITH EMPATHY

Today, at Tecomet, I'm working to spread this new perspective in every way that I can. I've always been a believer that one of the best qualities for a leader is empathy, and that is even more pronounced now because every decision we make from an employment perspective impacts someone's life and their family's life.

I've also had opportunities to apply that sense of empathy and understanding with the executive team here as we discussed how to approach conversations about race and equity with the broader team. In my value system, equality and social justice are among the top five values I have.

However, my husband helped me understand that sometimes these topics or concerns are just not part of someone else's life experience as much as they are mine. Thinking about that has made me more empathetic as well; people have different world views based on their own life experiences.

BETTER COMMUNICATION IS A KEY TO BETTER LEADERSHIP

I also believe that better communication is one of the keys to a stronger culture inside any company. I'm working on effective communication more and trying to coach my team in the importance of it. Everyone needs to ask better questions of each other, including some of the uncomfortable ones. For the people on my team, I'm asking more pointed and big-picture questions like, "What are you trying to accomplish? What's the end goal?" I've found that helps people get out of the weeds, take better feedback, and take things less personally.

For instance, someone on my team recently shared her frustration about a colleague who she felt was coming at her and making unfair statements, essentially pointing out some perceived failings on her part. I encouraged her not to just send long emails to the person debating every single point of her defense,

"PEOPLE HAVE DIFFERENT WORLD VIEWS BASED ON THEIR **OWN LIFE EXPERIENCES**" but to step back and look at what the critic was actually saying, then go back and have a conversation to understand why the person felt that way. High-performing teams understand this point: You have to recognize someone's intent. Recently I was struggling with a peer of mine, who seemed to be questioning my process and progress on a project, and I found myself jumping to conclusions, thinking that he was challenging me because he worried I wasn't on top of it, or that he couldn't trust me.

I found myself going down that path and then I realized I needed to pull myself back and say, well, have you asked him the question? So, I asked him the question. I told him up front that it wasn't my intention to damage our relationship or make any accusations, just that I was seeking to understand. And it was a really good dialogue. I understood then that he wasn't losing trust in me to follow through on the job. He was just feeling pressure to make sure it was visible to others that he was on top of it as well. We both came away with a better understanding of each other, and now we are in a new space.

At the end of the day, it's also helpful for leaders to think about the legacy they want to leave. It's not just about the results you've gotten—the revenue—but the legacy of how you've impacted people. I've thought about this since the day my kids were born, with my first child 30 years ago. They didn't care—and won't care—about what I did for a living. They only care about how I made them feel and who I was to them.

I think about that in terms of my work too—how do I want to make people feel? What's the legacy that I want to leave every day when I interact with the people on my team? It's not easy, and every day I'm far from perfect, but I'm also far less afraid to be who I am. And I sure hope they feel the same. ∎

THEY ONLY CARE ABOUT
HOW I MADE THEM FEEL

Alisa McGowan is Executive Vice President and Chief Human Resources Officer for Tecomet, which provides manufacturing solutions for the medical device and aerospace and defense markets. She has held leadership roles in human resources at a variety of companies, including Interface Performance Materials, Eastman Chemical Company, Rockwell Automation and Coca-Cola Enterprises.

CONTENTS

One lesson I've learned from a year of unprecedented change is that while a prevailing sense of uncertainty might be normal in times of crisis, it doesn't have to rule the day. There are concrete actions all leaders can take to turn worry and fear into defining moments for their organizations—moments that actually bring employees together in the best possible ways, and lift them up. I've seen many companies successfully navigate crisis over the past year and am convinced these strategies can help *ALL* leaders use their heart and head to successfully conquer difficult times. You'll find these strategies throughout the book, and you can also access our Proven Leader Tools, as described below.

ACCESS THE GROSSMAN GROUP'S PROVEN LEADER TOOLS

As a special add-on to help you lead and communicate even better in the future, *Heart First* readers have exclusive access to The Grossman Group's most sought-after and often-used leader tools. These are the same tools that have been licensed by dozens of Fortune 500 organizations, and are proven to work by saving you time and increasing your effectiveness. Look for the tools icon (top-left) throughout the book to know which tools are available for download. *See page 339 for information on how to download them.*

Q+As

FROM THE FRONT LINES

An unprecedented period of change led to remarkable insights from leaders at the top of their organizations. In these Q&As, they share more about what it takes to inspire teams in a time of crisis (and beyond).

THE CHANGE MAKERS

Throughout the book, meet an exceptional group of Change Makers—leaders at all levels who describe what exceptional leadership looks like.

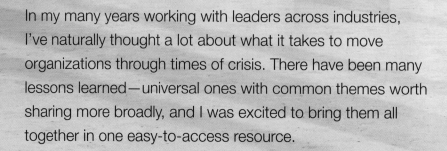

In my many years working with leaders across industries, I've naturally thought a lot about what it takes to move organizations through times of crisis. There have been many lessons learned—universal ones with common themes worth sharing more broadly, and I was excited to bring them all together in one easy-to-access resource.

But then something unexpected happened. A global pandemic quickly took over the world, forcing all of us to look at crisis and change in a completely new way. After all, it was the biggest level of change the world had experienced in more than a century. At the same time, the U.S.'s long history

of racial injustice came to the forefront in a way that can't be ignored. As I began interviewing leaders from a wide variety of organizations for their thoughts on how to lead through change, a common refrain emerged: "There's no playbook for how to lead through all this—we've had to make one up as we go."

I found that message profound and revealing. Intense periods of challenge and change require us to not just draw from experience, but also from what we know to be true in our gut. For me—and for many others I interviewed—the

most important lesson was about being human as we lead, what I call leading with heart. That soon became my guiding principle: What can we learn from this experience that helps us be better leaders with the humanity, courage and wisdom to carry our organizations forward in tough times as well as calmer ones? I kept coming back to this word—heart.

Over the past year—in such an unprecedented time of societal and economic upheaval—it was natural for leaders to feel powerless and anxious about the future at times. Especially in the early months of the pandemic, some leaders wondered how their business would survive, what the new normal would look like, and just what the COVID-19 pandemic would mean for their personal and professional lives. However, that sense of powerlessness didn't have to be the prevailing feeling. I saw many leaders using this challenging time as an opportunity to stand up and lead in moving ways. I was continually inspired by the concrete action leaders took to lead and communicate with heart—and guts. That is what this book is all about—applying those lessons learned to provide clear direction on how to be the very best leader and communicator you can possibly be.

One of my favorite quotes, from Martin Luther King Jr., offers much wisdom on this point. "The measure of a great person is not what they do in times of comfort and convenience, but where they stand at times of challenge." Let's face it: It's relatively easy to lead when times are good. It takes a lot more courage, grit and heart to lead during tough times.

Now more than ever, leaders play a pivotal role in connecting, calming and inspiring their teams. A big part of that is leading with

HEART F1RST

CHAPTER 1

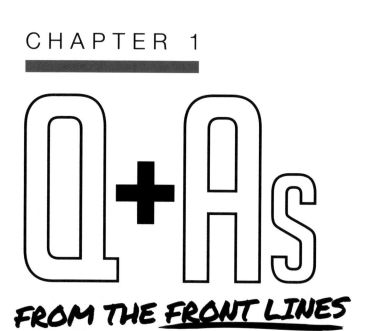

Q+As

FROM THE FRONT LINES

I sat down with some brilliant business leaders to get their front-line perspective on leadership during challenging times. They had some fascinating insights and practical advice that can work for many of us everyday.

Q+A WITH TAMER ABUAITA

SENIOR VICE PRESIDENT,
GLOBAL SUPPLY CHAIN, SC JOHNSON

I know you have a very interesting background and experience as an immigrant, which I'm sure shapes how you lead.

A Absolutely, and my life experience definitely influences the type of leader I aspire to be. The town in Egypt where I was born was extremely poor, with dirt roads and no infrastructure. It was just outside Cairo. My mother was a teacher at the local school and my dad was a salesman. We moved as a family to the U.S. with nothing. To survive, we had to earn our meal every day, literally struggle for every penny. I watched my parents work tirelessly to ensure their kids could survive, and they are shining examples of the value of hard work and what it takes to achieve your goals and dreams.

Because my family and I had nothing when we got to this country, I also appreciate everything, and deeply value diverse experiences and perspectives. After all, I have firsthand experience of the benefits of diversity. I've lived in Europe and called many parts of the U.S. home, including spots in California, Tennessee, Indiana, Pennsylvania, Florida and Illinois. Living in different places and being exposed to a broad diversity of people, beliefs, perspectives and business practices has helped me learn to listen and be open to looking at things in different ways. I know that what can seem unusual at first often turns out to be insightful and instructional. I've definitely learned that success is dependent on listening to and understanding differences if you want to deliver on the needs of your employees and consumers.

Is there a learning or two that you think has been especially important for you over the past year at SC Johnson?

A The past year felt like a telling moment that was going to define where I stood as a leader in the organization because it was the ultimate crisis, not only for our company but for the entire world. This is the type of moment where leaders of an organization are counted on the most to really show the character of a company.

I've been fortunate, though, because while I did not have a game plan going into this unprecedented time, I think we're a stronger company because of all the things that have happened to us and all that we've enabled as an organization. It definitely helps to be part of an organization that began as a family business and has grown to be a global leader by maintaining a focus on strong values and principles. Recently, I consulted with our human resources lead, David Whitman, and asked him to reflect back on the last year and share from a leadership perspective what we did well within the Supply Chain team and what we can work on.

That's great insight to pull from. What were the top learnings?

A David shared that we got some important things right early in the pandemic, in China. I got directly engaged very early at the working level to understand what was really going on there. By mid-January, we had heard about coronavirus hitting China and I realized that we needed to get on calls with these folks and hear what's going on and help them. So, I would get on calls every night from about 9pm until midnight, just talking to the team and understanding what they were facing. It was out of a sincere desire to help. But what was being watched by my leadership team and the broader organization was the idea that I wasn't delegating, but really getting involved and learning about what to do. When I turned around a month later and shared what we need to do in preparation for this crisis in the United States, I had first-hand knowledge of what folks were already going through in China.

INCOMING
CALL

MY LEARNING HERE IS THAT A CRISIS IS INDEED NOT A TIME TO DELEGATE.

You need to know what's going on at the ground level so you can better appreciate the challenges folks are dealing with. As an example, we had 16 employees in the Hunan Province when it was completely closed down due to COVID-19, as well as teammates whose family members were working in the Hunan Province. I learned that those employees' relatives couldn't even leave the street where they live, couldn't navigate from one area to another. All I could do was say: What can we do to help you? What can we do to reach out to your families? I put their personal lives and concerns first before I cared about what was going on with the factory.

When you think about an employee with a mother and father who can't leave their house, you've got to put yourself in their shoes, understand what they're going through, and ask them how you can help before you can even start to remotely think about what's happening with the business. I think that by getting involved at the working level, I helped set the tone for other leaders to also get involved at their own ground levels. It made it clear how important that was.

What else did you do early on to set the right tone?

A I think it was helpful that I immediately declared the priority in the first couple of meetings. I said: "The priority is the health and safety of our team. I don't care what else happens. Everyone better make sure that the priority is the health and safety of our team first and foremost in every decision we face."

I feel like I was lucky. Maybe it was a good day for me, but I was very clear on that point in China and that led to a principle for how we operated for the next several months until today, where everyone says, "Before we do anything, the health and safety of our team is first and foremost." That wasn't because it's a nice tagline or because we'd seen it anywhere else. It was because I genuinely cared about our folks.

PRIORITY

What kind of impact did that decision have?

A Attendance in all of our factories through the first several months of the pandemic was even better than it was before the crisis. We've cut our absenteeism in half because our actions helped employees feel safe at work. And when they feel safe at work and feel like work cares about them, they will show up and fight the good fight. And so the little statements early on really do matter. And I believe that leaders need to think about those statements, especially in times of crisis, because you're declaring your identity, your priority, and your focus in those statements. You just need to make sure that they're genuine and you can stand by them.

We've seen leaders state the opposite, that the focus is, "We need to get back to business," maybe not always so bluntly but that point is made before all others. Do you feel that backfires?

A To be fair, I can't say it was part of a grandiose plan, but because I had been on the ground level, understanding what people were worried about, I knew how concerned they were about their family members. That was top of mind before anything else. It would be naive of me to glaze over that importance and start talking only about the business results.

Was there a moment where the rubber met the road and that declaration created some challenges in terms of the business?

A Yes. China was naturally the first region to tackle this issue, and we saw the government saying at one point that it was time to bring folks back to work. We felt we had to make sure we had the right actions in place first so that employees felt they were going to a safe workplace. Without any other company in China doing this, to my knowledge, we immediately implemented the temperature protocols and the health and safety protocols. We brought in companies to disinfect on a regular basis. We invested millions of dollars of capital to create separation in a factory, and I would not allow anyone back in the factory until that happened. I made it mandatory to get that all done before anyone could come back.

Within five to six days, people moved mountains to implement all the things needed, and there was a lot of pressure swirling around us, with some saying, "Well, let's get folks in and then we'll deal with that on the fly." But we held true to the number one priority, which was safety. When the first wave of folks started coming back to the factory, word spread that employees were feeling energized, saying things like, "I love working here. Everything is safe. They care about my safety." Nobody else in the world was implementing temperature checks on January 18th. Of course, everyone

> YOUR SHOPPING CART

is doing it now, but I promise you that our team was among the very first to buy a temperature monitor in mid-January. And that was great because we got boatloads of them before the price went up!

This was all because I turned to our safety and health experts in the company and asked what we needed to do, and I gave them a voice. In China, that paved the way. The government came in and said we were the example of what others should do, and it became the beacon of excellence for the rest of the world, with all of our other locations implementing all of this last February 2020. In hindsight, that was the first test of whether it was just a sign on a wall or something we fundamentally felt. When employees saw we felt it, then they believed in it, too.

> PRODUCT REVIEWS

It sounds like the turning point for you was that your actions followed very quickly to demonstrate that you were sincere about keeping people safe.

A We started a line in six days. It probably would have taken six months otherwise. I believe it was because we set up a clear purpose for the team: We're keeping our family members and consumers safe. I know they were proud to say they accomplished this new line in six days.

It was good for your people, but do you think it was good for your business as well?

A Over the past year, our company has performed well. And the main reason was because our Supply Chain kept running without a beat, and even was producing more than it ever did.

Is there something new that you realized about yourself during this process?

A Yes, but I should share a little context first. I had to communicate often to the broader Global Supply Chain organization. In the early months of the pandemic, I was having town halls every three or four weeks with several thousand people. I would sit down to try to write notes and I couldn't, and I realized that I had to just talk to them about what was going on and be genuine about how I felt about it.

As I shared what was happening in different parts of the world, there would be a moment when I needed to share that a specific person had tested COVID positive, and I realized again that there's no script you can write for this. You just have to be very, very genuine. When you're genuine about how you feel and where you stand, then folks know they can trust you as a leader to take them through this unchartered time.

IT'S OKAY TO SAY 'I DON'T **KNOW'**

What I learned about myself was it was also okay to say, "I don't know where this is going. I don't know if I'm doing the right things and if we're doing the right things, but we're going to give it our best shot and we're going to learn through this together." I realized that it's not a sign of weakness to say, "I don't know," it's actually a sign of being genuine and that garners a certain amount of trust within the organization.

As I listen to you, there's the "I don't know" piece, but then there's also the strong idea that "We're going to figure this out together."

A Yes, I also think little things go a long way. Whenever anyone was out on quarantine during the early months of the pandemic, I personally called them no matter where they were around the world to check on them. Whenever I heard someone or their family member might have the symptoms or have a COVID positive test, I would call them to just check in.

I did that because I really cared about these folks. And I think word spreads and momentum spreads from those small things; it just naturally rubs off on others and they start doing the same. Then everybody worries about everyone else and it really brings the "We're in it together" mindset to life. Actions really matter. And no matter how small they are to you, they're huge to someone else.

CALLING
LORI

Is there anything you wished you had done differently in your early response to the pandemic?

A We didn't look for external points of view for any blind spots we could have been missing. We were so focused on what's going on today, but I could have asked more about what others were doing and what can we learn from. And while the Global Supply Chain team was ahead of everyone in SC Johnson on this and created an amazing nucleus, I think we could have done more to influence the broader organization by sharing our stories more and helping prepare them for what they were about to go through in our office locations.

This idea of how much you care, it's not a strategy of yours, but just who you are.

A I believe that it's people that make the difference in our company. We spend too much time at work and with too many people not to enjoy it and not to value the people who help us achieve what we want to achieve.

RECEIVE

What might hold some leaders back is the concern that empathy doesn't always lead to great business results. Is it your point that the two are one in the same—if you care, your business results will follow?

A I think that if you have an engaged team that is willing to break down walls for you, then inevitably the business will follow. And it's impossible to have an engaged team if they don't think you care about them and you value them and you are looking out for them and their families day in and day out. I think they're all interconnected in a way that ultimately will bring the business results as well. Yet at the end of the day, even if the business results didn't come, I had to be able to sleep at night and look at my kids and my family and be able to say, "I did the right thing by me." And so, for me, it was a no-brainer.

> I DID THE
> **RIGHT**
> THING BY ME

Tamer Abuaita is Senior Vice President, Global Supply Chain, at SC Johnson, a manufacturer of household cleaning products, home storage, air care, pest control and shoe care. Previously, he held leadership positions at The Kraft Heinz Company and Nestle.

Q+A WITH MATT SNOW

→ CEO, DHG

What do you think is most important to share about how to communicate in times of uncertainty and change?

A I've stayed very connected with a lot of other CEOs of similar firms across the country and we've all felt similarly— and the general feeling is, "Where's the playbook on how to run a firm in a global pandemic?" Unfortunately, there is not a playbook. As we began to navigate through these unchartered waters, I found it most helpful to remain true to the fundamentals of effective communication. We worked to provide timely, transparent, factual communications to our people. And, we worked to listen to our people by conducting frequent pulse surveys. The feedback provided by our people has definitely guided how we've operated.

How do you feel about your early response to the pandemic?

A The communication aspect of our response went well, and frankly has been one of the strategies that has allowed us to thrive. On Friday, March the 13th, we made the decision that we would completely close every office and that everybody would be working from home the following Monday morning. Our Executive Committee, the firm's governing body, said, "Matt, you've got to get in front of everybody, and you have to make them feel calm, that we have a plan in place, and that everything's going to be ok." And so I quickly learned that getting on a 2,200-person Zoom broadcast and just speaking the truth would be one of the most successful communication strategies for us. In the beginning, I was addressing our team members via Zoom once a week, when clarity and hope were needed the most. I think this approach brought us together and helped level set from the start.

How did the truth feel different in March than it did in January, and how did you begin to communicate and lead your team through that?

A At the end of February, we were on track to have a banner year, achieving a new level of $500 million in revenue. And quite literally in two weeks' time, that outlook changed. And so the message on my first Zoom broadcast was that we don't know what the future holds; however, we are a strong firm, and we are taking this one week at a time. I emphasized the need to stay connected to each other and to our clients as these connections would help us manage through operating in a virtual environment. We began sharing a theme with our people—"Emerge Strong." This theme really helped unite team members and worked as a rally cry during these challenging times.

PANDEMIC

That's a great theme. What context did you give to that theme?

 We had three principles underlying the theme:

1 We were taking care of our people first and making sure they are safe and have their needs met in adapting to the new ways of working.

2 We were taking care of our clients and their needs and staying in touch with them.

3 We were taking actions to maintain our financial strength to ensure we "Emerge Strong." We kept saying that week after week after week; the consistency of that message has kept our team together, so that we may be more cohesive and aligned today than we ever have been.

In your initial personal message to the entire team, did you share any of your own feelings of vulnerability or anything that was going on in your mind personally?

A Yes, a lot was going on in my own life at the time. When we made that decision to close, it was just a couple days after my dad had died of lung cancer. While we knew he was struggling, the timing was still a little unexpected.

And naturally, I was pretty vulnerable on Tuesday morning when I spoke to everyone. I said I just want to thank you all for supporting me, and I said I'm sure you all have other things going on in your lives too—concerns with family members, how you're going to make rent, or what you're going to do during the day with your kids at home. And so I said that part of us being strong and resilient here is just to do our best in spite of what we have going on in our lives.

Have you always felt that way in your career—that it's ok to share your own challenges as a leader in times of change?

A Yes, I believe leaders need to be believable and credible. You have to be vulnerable because we're all human. And it's not just being vulnerable about the challenging things in your life. The lighthearted personal feelings are good to share too. In that very first Zoom call after we closed our offices, I pulled my dog up and I said, "This is Ruby and she is wondering why we're all here at home because this has rocked her world." We had some funny things like that going on.

I agree Matt, and I think that it's powerful to say, 'I'm trying to understand where you're coming from and I care.' And I also believe that there's just something so freeing and empowering to speak one's truth, whether it's as an individual or on behalf of the organization.

A You're right. It's important to acknowledge the truth whenever possible. For instance, we all realized that after a month, this pandemic reality was not going away quickly, and life was not returning to normal anytime soon. There was a true mental health element to our circumstances in addition to the many other factors. And so on one of my calls, we invited in Brooks Gallagher. He's a clinical psychologist and a former principal in our firm focused on coaching and organizational health. He shared coping skills to help our team members with more personal, mental health challenges that people were likely experiencing. And then we brought him in again later to help us deal with the fact that we were having salary cuts and having to furlough team members.

What other supports helped you get through the challenges team members were feeling?

A Jeff Outten, our director of change management, has been invaluable. We brought him on board about three years ago; I don't know what we would have done without him, because this pandemic has been the ultimate change that we experienced together. He has been such a solid check on so many things that I have done and communicated.

> **HAVING A LASER FOCUS ON CHANGE AGILITY AND REFERRING BACK TO OUR CHANGE MANAGEMENT PRINCIPLES WERE STEPS THAT REALLY HELPED US.**
>
> ☰

Are there any other things you wished you had done differently if given the chance?

A We really were unprepared for the adverse impact on working parents and especially our women professionals. I think in many households, women end up with the lion's share of childcare. I don't mean that as a blanket statement, but unfortunately that's primarily what we saw.
The reality is that we had trouble with all working parents being able to balance it all. I think I would have started out a little differently and thought more about how to help working parents manage through all of this if we had to do it over again. The other thing that we didn't do well was scenario planning. I'm thinking about a recent edition of *Harvard Business Review*; they discussed scenario planning and how effective the U.S. Coast Guard was in scenario planning and how much it really helped secure the country after 9/11. I realized we didn't do enough scenario planning, and I would like to have done that more.

BREAKING NEWS ALERT ❯

What other challenges has your firm faced since the pandemic began?

A We started March 16th working virtually, and we entered into a lockdown mode across our footprint. We thought, 'We're so glad we don't have anything else going on.' And then we saw the events involving Breonna Taylor, Ahmaud Arbery and George Floyd. I soon realized that in fact we do have something else major going on, and I needed to get in front of our Black team members and talk about this. We needed to deal with this second crisis quickly. I don't know that some of us have ever worked so hard. We have been spending as much time focused on racial injustice as we have been on managing the firm through the pandemic. When we are faced with crisis issues that run to the core of the firm, as leaders, we have no choice but to roll up our sleeves and get the work done. We figure out how to make it happen.

What was the truth you shared to begin the dialogue on racial injustice?

A Fortunately, we had started the dialogue during the fall partner meeting, showing statistics demonstrating that our team member experience varies greatly based on race. If you're white, pretty much everything's going great. If you're a minority—and I specifically carved out Black team members—you have a very different experience. Of course nobody sets out intending for this, but it's what the data shows. One speaker also highlighted the changing demographics in our country and how that will impact the future of our firm; we did a livestream of his presentation for the entire firm.

The truth that we highlighted was that our Black team members are hurting due to systemic racism, which manifested itself at DHG (and frankly, probably at most other companies in the country as well) in the form of unconscious bias. And we talked very openly about it. We did an interview with one of our Black partners who helped us talk through it. And then we did another panel discussion where our leader of inclusion and diversity talked about the experience of being Black in America and at DHG. As I reflect, this was probably more impactful than anything we'd done with our colleagues up to that point.

What was the reaction from the full team?

A There was something cathartic about it. For those who are Black, there was this feeling of, 'Oh, I can finally talk about this.' And for other team members, there were opportunities to ask uncomfortable questions. We divided team members into smaller groups of 35 people or less and held what we call Unity Workshops to facilitate dialogue and sharing. We received overwhelmingly positive feedback on these sessions. And we learned a lot about each other and the world around us. I applaud the work our HR team did to plan and facilitate

60+ WORKSHOPS AROUND THE FIRM.

What made you decide to actually have those candid sessions? It had to be a little nerve wracking to put yourself out there like that.

A It definitely made us feel vulnerable, but it was the right thing to do. What convinced us to do it was having conversations with our Black professionals and team members all over the firm. Through just a couple of phone calls asking them what they thought about what was going on, they shared that we really needed to talk about current events and racial injustice.

IT WAS THE RIGHT THING TO DO

Any other final words on learnings from leading through a crisis?

 Going through a global pandemic, paired with racial injustice, has highlighted for me the importance of personal communication, being transparent and telling the truth. What I learned from the pandemic and from that first candid conversation on March the 16th helped me sooner than I expected when we later initiated the conversations about racial injustice just a few months later.

MAKE COMMUNICATION PERSONAL

Headquartered in Charlotte, NC, DHG is among the top 20 public accounting firms in the nation. In more than 30 years in public accounting, **Matt Snow** has worked with a wide range of clients, from start-ups to large national organizations. He is passionate about talent development and enjoys mentoring others in the profession. Leading his firm of more than 2,000 professionals across the U.S. and in the United Kingdom, Matt says he has never faced a more challenging time than in the months following the COVID-19 pandemic and the racial unrest around the country. Both incidents have led to many candid conversations about how best to address employee needs and further enhance the work culture at DHG.

Q+A WITH DAN COSTELLO

CEO, HOME RUN INN

As the CEO of a frozen pizza and restaurant business with locations around Chicago, you've faced a number of challenges over the past year, including violent protests outside businesses in Chicago. How are you doing and how is your team doing?

A Given everything, we're doing well, and the business is doing well. I think part of the reason we've been successful through this crisis is we've spent a lot of time over the past several years focusing on our values as a company, and trying to help our teams and our business leaders understand what it means to live our values. We relied on that during the pandemic as we had to make very tough decisions that impacted the health and safety of our workforce as well as our customers. For me, that helped because I felt very intentional in the decisions we made.

OUR VALUE FOR FAMILY GUIDED
EVERYTHING

For instance, there was a time early in the pandemic when we had to consider whether to close our manufacturing plant that produces frozen pizzas. When you close a plant for the day, that costs several thousands in sales that we won't get back, but that doesn't mean it isn't the right thing to do in certain situations. As a food producer, we were an essential business and were allowed to continue operating despite state and city shutdown orders.

Still, early in the pandemic, there was a lot of anxiety among employees and we understood that many were wondering if they should still come to work. As we considered what to do, I turned to our company values—which center on an appreciation of our family of employees. Our value for family guided everything we did. So that meant we closed the plant for 2½ days in March to allow time to think through our processes and address the concerns of employees. When you're able to make a decision like that with clear intention, you can communicate it better, and you do it with confidence.

In the past when you've faced tough decisions, do you think you communicated more impulsively?

A We've made decisions in the past that felt like last-minute decisions and I sometimes felt forced into them, like I had to react right away. And when you work from a reactive state, it's easy to put out an announcement or initiative that isn't as well thought out and doesn't consider how your team might respond or how it might impact everyone. But when you can actually be intentional about it and thoughtful, then your communication can be that much more impactful. And for me, the added benefit of that is I can speak with more confidence.

Recipe · · *Ingredients*

I understand you also made the personal decision to work alongside your employees when the plant re-opened. As CEO, you could have just managed everything from the office. Why did you do that, especially given that you have five kids at home and probably worried about putting them—and your wife—at risk?

A Philosophically for me, it's hard to ask other people to do something you're not willing to do yourself. Later in the summer, I got back to my normal routine with more time in the office. But during those opening weeks and months, I tried to be on the floor much more than I have in the past. I was just trying to support people, basically saying, "If you're here, I'm going to be here."

One of the other reasons I felt compelled to do this was for the benefit of our full team of employees. There were financial ramifications for the company, but also for the employees. I was fortunate to not have anyone in my immediate family with risk factors or underlying health conditions; otherwise, my decision might have been different. My wife Julie was supportive and my family was supportive, so that gave me the ability to do that.

IF YOU'RE HERE, I'M GOING TO BE HERE

In those early days when so much was unknown and there were so many concerning stories, that was a brave decision. Did you ever reconsider that choice?

A When we found out about the first one or two positive cases of workers in the plant, I naturally thought more about it. I wasn't even worried about myself but wondered about my kids, like what if one of them had an underlying condition that I didn't even know about. So I was definitely worried about it. My wife slept in a different room for a couple months. I would come home, put my clothes in the washer, and immediately take a shower. But that feeling also helped me be even more empathetic with the team, recognizing how they must have felt and the risks they were taking to come to work every day.

What do you think your team would say that you did well during that time?

A I think the thing they were most grateful about was the fact that we would tell them exactly what was going on. We didn't withhold information about cases or anything. I feel like that was even more impactful for them than us being down there working with them. I spent several mornings at the plant before we officially opened just filling them in on everything that I could: This is what we're doing with pay rates, this is what we think about masks, this is what we'll do to take temperatures, etc. And also why we're doing all of this—to keep everyone safe. That kind of constant and thorough communication helped to build trust in the way we were managing things.

In addition to the pandemic, there were clear concerns with violence and protests in the city over the George Floyd killing. How did you respond to that?

A I was asked to make a public statement and I thought about it and ultimately declined to make an immediate, kneejerk type statement. I wanted to be guided by the right intentions, and not just react just to say something. One of the things I learned during the crisis was that nobody can communicate for me on matters as important as that. So, we decided instead to start by really trying to understand what our role should be and how we might help lead in this area. I wanted us to reflect and look at ourselves first, in an objective way, and have the important discussions internally. For instance, it would have been easy to say that we've got five women general managers leading our nine restaurants and two are Black women and two are Hispanic males, so that means we're diverse, right? That would have been simple to do. But instead, I wanted us to actually take the time to ask what has our progress been and what more do we need to do? So that's what we're trying to do now.

Where has that led you so far?

A We started to have more discussions asking minorities and people of color what their experience has been like working for us. And we brought in some outside experts to discuss unconscious bias with our full team. Eventually I think the reflections we're doing now will get us to a real vision for what we're going to do and be able to put a stake in the ground on this issue. That's more important than me writing some reactive statement when we don't even know if we're living up to it yet. I believe you have to understand where your organization is first and know who you are and what you want to accomplish.

What else did you learn about leading in this time of change?

A I've seen even more the importance of communication. David, you always say that whether you're openly communicating, or saying nothing, you're always communicating something. I understand that even more now. When the pandemic began, I started a weekly update for the company, something we've never done before. We communicated on various categories: The team's health; what's going on in our industry generally with manufacturing and in the restaurants; and how is the pandemic impacting our business. Then we always conclude it by describing the things we're most focused on.

We also got into a much better rhythm with our meetings and we made more space to have weekly executive team meetings and other regular meetings for the various functions. Before it was much more sporadic and less efficient. Again, I would use the word intentional. We're being a lot more intentional about how we meet and when we meet and the purpose of our meetings, and that has allowed us to communicate better during this whole time.

Given all that you've learned during the last several months of unprecedented change, what would you advise new leaders?

A The most important thing is that you have to understand the role you play in developing trust. If you just expect trust, I think that would be an error. You have to work at it and you really have to understand how important creating trust with someone is. If you can't build trust, you can't get anything done. Additionally, you want to be guided by intention and meaningful values.

You have to be really specific about what you want the workplace to look like, how you want leaders and employees to act. It's important as leaders to constantly ask: What is my intention? Are you oriented toward yourself and making yourself look better, or are you oriented toward others? If you can show that you're credible, oriented toward helping others, and you do what you say you're going to do, then you can build trust. Without a focus on how all of that comes in, I don't know that you can lead change.

Dan Costello is CEO of Home Run Inn Pizza, a fourth-generation family-owned Chicago-area restaurant company that also owns and operates two factories, supplying frozen pizzas to retailers in more than 40 states. Dan has worked more than 25 years helping to define and develop Home Run Inn's brand and strategy, and is now responsible for the strategic direction of the restaurant and manufacturing divisions. He is also an active member of the Young Presidents Organization and serves on the Board of Directors of the Illinois Restaurant Association and the Management Association of Illinois.

Q+A

WITH VICTOR SWINT

PRESIDENT AND CEO, TECOMET

You've obviously faced many challenges in 2020. Is there a key learning you've had about leadership during this tumultuous time?

A A big learning is an understanding of the power and importance of communication. With all that's going on with the pandemic and this awful racial divide that we're dealing with, it has been really clear that people needed a better linkage to our team. They needed to understand daily what we were doing and our perspective. Through better communication, I think we've helped our employees see that we are genuinely concerned about their well-being and we're doing everything we can to keep everybody safe. I think that message has come across loud and clear.

I also think they've seen that our company stands for justice and respect and believes in making all of our lives better. We have regularly scheduled employee meetings and town halls as a way of letting our employees know where we stand, and the values we believe in. In all of that work, we focus on creating a bridge for genuine and open dialogue, and it's ongoing.

How do you use communication to improve your culture?

A Well before the pandemic, we had been working a lot on shaping a culture for a different kind of company. I think that's really helped us manage all the changes around us today. One of our top priorities is building a culture and team where everyone feels they can be their best selves at work, respected and valued for their ideas and welcomed and included because of their diverse backgrounds and perspectives. This is important for our customers because it helps us understand their needs better and innovate. It's also important to me personally—on a human level—because I want Tecomet to be the gold standard for what a work experience can be. A big part of that is not being constrained by hierarchy.

I welcome ideas from everywhere in the company. Rank and titles shouldn't determine who's at a meeting. Instead, I want each person to know they can make a difference and feel empowered and encouraged to contribute. In some parts of the organization, this may seem like seismic change. In other parts, maybe we're closer to this vision.

When you started communicating more about the culture you're working to build, what kind of reaction did you get from your team?

A Our focus on communicating more definitely paid off. In the past, we'd had very little dialogue at meetings and barely any questions. But once we really started to emphasize genuine dialogue, the mood shifted. Now you have to stop the meeting and take questions to answer afterwards because there are so many, and they're all thoughtful and constructive questions. And I've tried to keep rewarding the honest dialogue, telling team members to tell me how and why I may be wrong with a certain point of view. And as people open up and share tough questions, I know that raises awareness of issues that we have not even known existed before.

ONCE WE EMPHASIZED GENUINE DIALOGUE, THE MOOD **SHIFTED**

As a Black CEO, what is the most important idea you want to teach about racial equality in the world of work?

A I believe leadership in a corporation needs to be about more than profitability. Leadership is also about working to make the world a better place, which I believe is about creating an environment where all ideas are heard. That also means there needs to be inclusion. And I definitely think senior leaders like myself need to hold themselves accountable and own this issue personally. Just as we own sales and value creation and executing for the company, we should own the creation of an environment that supports equity in the workplace.

What specifically have you shared with your team on the topic of racial justice concerns?

A I shared with them that despite my feelings of occasional despair, I remain an optimist. Protest itself is an optimistic act, a belief that things can be better when we all try to engage. I also challenged our entire team to embrace the hard work of becoming a better, more inclusive and empathetic group. The clear message was that at Tecomet, we cannot ignore the world around us, and we don't want to. Instead, we want to be a force for good. We're dedicated to healing, and that should include the damage and scars caused by our current world. I believe that like any high performing team, we are stronger because of our differences—because we have varied experiences, styles, backgrounds and perspectives.

PROTESTS
ROCK NATION

THE CONVERSATION MOVES US FORWARD

FASTER

Do you find yourself using your voice more on this sensitive issue, not just with employees but in other venues?

A I feel like I'm a lot more fearless on this issue right now. In part it's the time we're in. I feel like this is a time when people are reaching out to me and they want to know what I'm going to do. There's an expectation and a need, and that has led me to be more fearless than in the past.

Before, I was always worried that people were going to look at what I said on this issue and see it as self-serving. And I wondered if it would be one more thing that would make it harder for me to fit in, or keep me from becoming one of the team, so to speak. So in the past, I spent time creating a high performance team and a mission, vision, and values that supported people to do their best work, and eventually that led to diversity. But now I'm speaking out much more about my own experiences and what it looks like on the other side, and I think the conversation moves us forward faster.

How has that felt for you, to raise your voice even more?

A It's opened up a can of worms personally because emotions that I haven't felt for a long time have surfaced. As a business person, things happen that you just rationalize and you move on because you don't want to dwell on it. But now, I've had this pattern of reflection. I was almost embarrassed when it came on. Like if you'd asked me three or four months ago what kind of racism I experienced, I would have struggled to answer.

But now I remember all of it, like walking down the street and heading from the Boston Garden and being called the N word by four guys. I was told to go home where I came from, referencing Africa even though I'm an American. Some of the other disturbing events that have happened in my career have also surfaced in my memory, and I've reflected on how they impacted me at the time.

What is it that you'd like others to know about what it's like to be a Black American today in corporate America?

A There's a broader question of just what it's like to be a Black American first, and the point is that Black Americans love our country. We don't want to leave the country. Instead, we want the country to live up to the ideals that it has long stood for. We're at this period that now we have more information, and we're seeing all these pictures and the totality of everything that is happening and it's moving not just Black Americans, but all Americans to want to change things, and recognize that if some of us aren't free, none of us are free.

What does all of this mean for African Americans in a work environment? What I hope it means is that we can all be more fearless and bring our true selves to the office, whether it's hairstyles or dress or generally how we interact with people. It's this idea that I'm going to put it out there and be my best self and hope that the organization is willing to work with that and not feel like I have to be a carbon copy of someone else. I think about my own career; I did everything I thought I had to do to fit in and move up. I went to Harvard business school. I played golf, not because I felt like I needed to, but because I felt like I had to be able to check all the boxes, that somehow if I didn't, I wasn't going to make it. So I hope that is changing and that it's going to be better for Black Americans in the future.

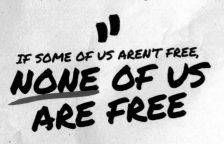

IF SOME OF US AREN'T FREE,
NONE OF US ARE FREE

There's a lot of discussion among leaders and employees now, but what actions are needed for real change to happen when it comes to a more diverse and inclusive workforce?

A What I hope is that the discussions on race lead to more diversity on the board of directors of corporate boards. If we can we get more diversity on the board, then everything else is going to fall into place because the board is then going to push for diversity, ethics and accountability.

So I hope corporate boards are willing to step up and put metrics in place and hold everybody accountable and be willing to take the company through the journey. That will really move the needle on this very critical issue.

> I HOPE CORPORATE BOARDS ARE WILLING TO **STEP UP**

Victor Swint is President and Chief Executive Officer of Tecomet, a medical device manufacturer of orthopedic implants, instruments and sterilization cases. Prior to joining Tecomet, Victor spent more than 20 years in various manufacturing organizations, serving as the CEO of Interface Performance Materials, a Group President at Illinois Tool Works, and Vice President and General Manager at Rockwell Automation, among other roles.

JULY 4, 1776.

States of

Q+A
WITH RICH STODDART

→ FORMER CEO, INNERWORKINGS, INC.

You faced a lot of challenges in 2020. You not only had the pandemic to wrestle with, but you were also leading InnerWorkings through a critical turnround period, with the company ultimately being acquired by another firm. What are some of your general observations and reflections on the challenges for leading through such a pivotal time of change?

A   I can boil my high-level thoughts down to three things. First, just communicate. We did a weekly webcast with all employees for quite a long time, and that was in direct reaction to the fact that people simply needed to "be together" because of the isolation. Next, as a leader, don't pretend that you have all the answers. That was initially difficult for me, as I would think it would be for most leaders. Likewise, we made a commitment to transparently saying on certain issues and questions "we don't know, but when we know something more, we will tell you." Third, I found it important to be vulnerable, and let people know that I too was feeling unsettled and uncertain, which I know can also be counterintuitive for most leaders.

Probably the best decision I made was that we were not going to do much communication via email and instead use video. It was about being seen and being consistent; the sessions we had were attended by roughly 70 percent of our employees on a weekly basis, and they were also much less structured than what we would normally do. It really came down to being real—which is actually one of our values—all the time. It was great to let people see that we were all in basically the same boat and while we were taking decisive actions as leaders to do what was best for the company and our people, we weren't sure what might happen next.

..ill 📶   100% 🔋

How did you decide to move away from email, at least initially?

A We did send some communication out at first in email. But when I saw and experienced myself this sense of isolation and disconnection, email simply seemed too transactional. People didn't want to know policies; they wanted to know if they were going to be ok. And it became very clear to me that we needed to honor what people were feeling. The webcast allowed us to have much more of a dialogue and it felt like we were becoming more of a family— supporting one another and talking about what we were feeling.

You've mentioned the importance of showing vulnerability, so let's talk about your own leadership in these times. What's something you learned about yourself as a leader?

A I come back to this idea that as a leader, you don't need to have all the answers. You can make good, smart decisions without all the answers. Importantly, that was not how I had been "trained" as a leader or what my previous experience was.

I realized that you can still be thoughtful and pragmatic, work various possibilities and scenarios, but in times of great change, some things simply won't be known and you need to move ahead regardless. That concept of taking a "leap of faith" became very real for me. I learned that it was ok to make educated guesses and go with your gut feeling. There was less time to weigh the pros/cons of decisions, too.

Can you share an example of a time when you went with more of this "gut feeling"?

A An example that comes to mind is that we were scheduled to do a webcast for employees two days after the death of George Floyd. When I heard the news, I said we need to do something different. I didn't necessarily know what that was, but the content that we had planned and prepared needed to change. When my staff said I should moderate a panel, I declined. I said that as a white man in a position of power that seemed to reinforce my position of power and privilege, so I said I would participate as a panelist rather than make this "my" meeting.

We ended up doing a panel on racism with some external resources we had tapped into during Black History Month. We had quite a "raw" discussion, including my own admission that several generations back, my family in Arkansas had owned slaves. I had never said that before in a public setting, and it felt cathartic. It's also important to note here that this was an organization that really hadn't focused on diversity and inclusion much at all previously. So, this conversation was quite new and different for our employees. It ended up kickstarting a lot of energy around all of our employee resource groups as well.

"IT *FELT* CATHARTIC"

What were some of the concerns with opening up a discussion on diversity and inclusion?

A Diversity and inclusion issues are always challenging and made more so by only being able to get together virtually. We are at a moment where we have situations with no answers on top of situations with no answers, which really puts leaders to the test. But, I've learned and now have a much greater appreciation for the value of talking and listening as an important first step when you are not sure what might be the best route to take.

*It sounds like this built within the organization a place
to say what had perhaps previously been unspeakable?*

A Well, yes, I would say the barrier for people between work and home
was broken down and I think that was a "good" thing. People could be
more of their authentic selves, bring the whole person that they are to
the work they do on behalf of the company. And my sense is that this will lead
to less stress ultimately and likely higher levels of trust, which is what we've
been looking for in organizations for a long time. So, it's unfortunate that we've
had to live through a pandemic and a reckoning with the systemic social
injustice for it to happen, but now I'm hoping we can start to see the benefits
of trust, such as greater collaboration, productivity, creativity and innovation.
Going forward, I think organizations will be healthier places overall and will be
places people want to stay and put forth their best efforts.

---

*You mentioned you had recently rolled out some core values.
How did these factor into managing all the change?*

A It was a very interesting experience. We had just launched and had been
working with the senior leadership team on the values right before the
pandemic started. Then, what would probably normally be a several year
process with videos training, work sessions, etc. became an organic process; it just
happened naturally. We were living the values because we had to live the values.

What had been designed as very operational naturally shifted to being guideposts
for action. The values spoke directly to how you should show up. The four values
we defined—"be real, stronger together, bring energy, and find a better way"—really
helped people know what to do and how to behave. So, I really think it emphasizes
the importance of writing values that are more than nice words or phrases. Values
need to be concrete; they can't be things that sit off to the side or on a shelf.

I know going forward, I am going to double down on the importance of building a
strong culture and putting values in place with speed and vigilance. Without clearly
defined values, an organization will be ill prepared in a time of crisis.

I think some of the wisest words I've heard came from a leader I met early in my career. He said that if you get the behaviors right, everything else follows.

A Agreed. What I've said to those who remain at the company is to hold onto those values, keep the fire burning. There was something really special we were doing pre the acquisition with the behaviors we were living into, and your job is to keep it alive.

KEEP THE FIRE BURNING

Rich Stoddart is an accomplished Chief Executive Officer with extensive experience leading global organizations. He began his career at Leo Burnett, where he ultimately served as CEO of one of the world's largest advertising agencies. Most recently, he led a comprehensive transformation of InnerWorkings, Inc., (INWK). Under his leadership, a new operational focus and financial discipline were instituted that led to significant profitability improvements, while at the same time achieving record new business awards. InnerWorkings was sold in October 2020 to its largest competitor, backed by Blackstone.

Q+A WITH JEFF WINTON

> CEO, JEFF WINTON ASSOCIATES

You have an interesting background as a corporate communications leader guiding an organization through change and moments of crisis. In fact, one of your first major corporate communications roles was during the AIDS crisis in the 1980s. What are some of the biggest leadership lessons from that role?

A As a young gay man living in New York City in the 1980s, I had a lot of friends impacted by HIV and AIDS, obviously one of the biggest health crises to hit our country. Many friends are sadly no longer around because of the AIDS crisis. Living through that inspired me to volunteer in the AIDS community. I had the opportunity to get involved in a couple different nonprofit groups, including one that paired you with a person living with HIV or AIDS, and you became their advocate by taking them to doctors' appointments or anything else they needed. I was assigned to a family where three generations of the family were living with AIDS—the grandmother, the daughter, and the young son. My work as an advocate ultimately caught the attention of Roche, a Swiss company that was one of the early leaders in HIV and AIDS drug treatment.

Roche needed someone to come in and be a voice within the company for the AIDS community. That was my first foray into pharma. I had to quickly learn HIV and AIDS from a business standpoint. I knew it as a volunteer, but that was it. And as I look back on it now, that was probably one of the best jobs I've ever had because on a day-to-day basis, I was working directly with people who were benefiting from the biopharmaceutical industry.

As a leader, did you share your experience as a gay man who had personally lost friends?

A I remember after I began this job, I was talking to a person who worked for one of the company's PR agencies and he was openly gay. I told him, "The company doesn't know my story, but the community does. I'm worried about this being career suicide if I'm too open about it, at least to start." And he looked at me and said, "Jeff, you're going to have instant credibility with the AIDS community if you level with them and freely let them know that. You're sharing that 'I'm one of you, I've been there, and I've had friends who died.'" He told me I had an obligation to "be who you are," and that lesson has never left me. After all those years of hiding and pretending to be somebody I wasn't, to finally be able to be who I am, and not to have to worry about it, I realize that's a big deal.

What other early lessons did you learn about leadership during challenging times as it relates to communication?

A A former CEO I worked for asked me to share some honest feedback about something following a meeting. At the time, I was in a junior communications role, and not sure how candid I should be. I remember distinctly that he said, "Tell me how people are really doing. I'm being told one thing but all too often when you're CEO, people sugarcoat things, and they tell you what you want to hear," So, I tried to be an honest guy as I always do. At the end of that conversation, the leader said, "Will you agree to meet with me on a monthly basis? My senior leaders are telling me what they think I want to know. If I'm going to be effective as a CEO, I need to know what's really happening." I think there's an important lesson there for leaders, both during "normal" times and in the midst of a crisis. You just need to have people around you who keep you grounded, who keep you real and keep your feet on the ground.

Growing up on a modest farm in Western New York helps keep me focused on the importance of candid conversations as well. I realize now, many years later, that while my parents weren't college educated and didn't have much money, they taught me things that no Ivy League education could have ever taught me. And truth is one of those. That's what keeps me focused and keeps me grounded.

AIDS RESEARC

You launched your own communications agency, Jeff Winton Associates, during a very tumultuous time over the past year. What have been some of your biggest recent learnings?

A It has certainly been an interesting and challenging year. We had just officially launched my new firm before the pandemic began. Fortunately, almost everyone had worked together in previous lives. So, we were in a pretty good position to move into the health crisis. It became clear very quickly, however, that people were missing actual human contact and interaction. I also personally learned that I would "burn out" if I did too many back-to-back online meetings. I needed time after a meeting to reset emotionally and I needed to allow extra time for meetings because it was clear quite soon that most people simply needed to talk and not necessarily about business, especially in those early days.

As the situation evolved, some "truths" emerged that many of us probably knew intuitively and acted on as part of being a leader. The health and social justice issues reinforced the importance of listening with empathy and for understanding as well as the critical need for getting intentional feedback about how employees are feeling and what they need. In particular, knowing how employees want to be communicated with and what information they desired was really important.

In working with other companies, what else did you see that worked well, and what needed improvement?

A There's a really important role that the overall culture plays during this time. Organizations that had previously established high levels of trust, engagement and respect for multiple points of view have faired better than others in continuing to move productively forward. The good news is that I have also seen others pivot to make changes to enhance their organizations' culture relative to listening and acting with authenticity, honesty, and respect for multiple viewpoints. Now, the key will be to sustaining these kinds of cultures. Carefully reflecting on our lessons learned and maintaining a level of "organizational memory" that doesn't permit a slide back to the old ways of thinking and acting will be critical. Reverting back to the old days likely won't be possible, but more importantly could be harmful to the positive course that has been initiated.

"
OUR ABILITY
TO RESPOND AND
MOVE
AHEAD
IS ESSENTIAL

From a personal perspective, how have you managed 2020?

A   In the midst of it all, I experienced two brain hemorrhages requiring emergency surgery just weeks after launching the firm, and this was a bit of a wake-up call about my own self-care. My own situation brought into crisper focus my abilities to work effectively when things are "gray" or unknown. Growing up on a farm where you face unpredictable situations all the time, such as too little or too much rain, or a windstorm that blows away your crops, and on and on. What my early years taught me is that there are many things we can't really control. I think that helped my ability to accept the ambiguity and be ok with not being sure about the future.

Of course, it wasn't ideal that my personal health issues ran parallel to the worldwide pandemic. Yet oddly, because of my background, not knowing what would happen next was almost second nature to me. I consider this ability to stay focused on the future without really knowing what it might be to be one of my leadership strengths. And I would submit that this ability is one that I think all leaders should try to build. If we've learned nothing else in recent times, it's that situations beyond our control can and will occur so our ability to respond and move ahead is essential.

Was there anything that surprised or impressed you about your team's response during these challenging times?

A What both crisis situations brought to the forefront were the people who could be counted on, who were willing to step up and go above and beyond what might have been expected. I think it is important to recognize those people for their supportive efforts. And, particularly in organizations, to take their actions into consideration for future development opportunities. I believe in the importance of not taking anything or anyone for granted. My own situation and the pandemic have been stark reminders of the fleeting nature of our existence. More than ever, prioritizing your time around what is truly important—that age-old work and life balance—is how we can be most successful in the future.

What characteristics have you identified about successful leaders in 2020?

A Again, resilience in the face of uncertainly can't be overstated. Likewise, a willingness to show vulnerability and humanness is at the core of creating trust within an organization. As a leader, you don't always have all the answers and you don't need to. We've had the chance to witness firsthand that most employees want authenticity. Having the courage to listen with an open mind and without a specific agenda is also quite important. Listening simply to listen is what is needed for effective leadership. Particularly in challenging situations, leaders need to find a way to step into uncomfortable places, take feedback from people at all levels of the organization, and keep going back for more information and feedback.

ALL OF THIS SHOULD BE CONSIDERED AN **UNENDING LOOP**

THIS KIND OF ACTIVITY ISN'T SOMETHING WE ONLY DO FOR A WHILE OR FOR A PROJECT; IT NEEDS TO BE EMBEDDED INTO THE CULTURE.

What connection do you see in leading with heart internally and externally?

A I think the same principles actually apply for both internal and external audiences. It's openness, it's about asking, it's about listening and then following through. Any organization needs to say: Do we know how our employees want to be communicated with? What's most important to them? It's also true for shareholders, clients, the media, whoever your audiences are. Through it all, you need to be asking the tough questions, namely: How does the organization need to change based on what we learn and what happens if we don't change?

Yes, it's hard work, and yes, we may not like all the answers. But I believe it's worth it. I am encouraged by the numbers of organizations I am seeing and hearing about following this path. If there is a silver lining to all we have faced, it may be that we will end up with a more human, authentic, life-affirming approach to communications.

Jeff Winton is the Chief Executive Officer of Jeff Winton Associates, a corporate affairs and communications agency. He has a four-decade communications and corporate affairs career with both leading corporations and respected public relations and advertising agencies. His global experience spans highly diverse and dynamic industries, including the pharmaceutical, biotechnology, animal health, agricultural and consumer arenas. Prior to founding his namesake agency, Winton was Senior Vice President of Public Affairs at Alkermes in Boston, served as Senior Vice President of Corporate Affairs at Astellas Pharma, and held numerous other roles in corporate communications.

Q+A

WITH EVAN SWIDLER

→ CHIEF PEOPLE OFFICER, IRI

CARE ENOUGH TO BUILD A TRULY DYNAMIC CULTURE

All companies today face some tough questions about the need for a more inclusive culture. What can you share about the company vision inside IRI?

A As a fundamental starting point, building an inclusive culture, recognizing that every employee is unique in their needs, is simply the right thing to do. Our Diversity, Equity and Inclusion (DEI) philosophy statement makes this clear—"We believe in the undeniable strength that diverse people, culture, thought and skill bring to our business, our clients, our people, and our communities. We are committed to building that kind of dynamic culture, one that embraces and celebrates openness, collaboration, creativity, equity, inclusivity, and growth."

Naturally, though, that statement is simply not enough. However, it is an essential guiding philosophy and critical foundation from which we build every day. We recognize that we have to live up to it. We've been working diligently to connect with our employees over the last year to understand how they're feeling. Making progress has to start with actually hearing what our employees have to say and then empowering them to be part of the solution and effect change for IRI or the communities we work with. To that end, we've had 30+ listening sessions with employees, so we're not making assumptions about what they're thinking, but instead listening to understand their needs and our opportunities to evolve.

A core building block to making progress focuses on building awareness and know-how on the subject. As a starting point, we've launched an Unconscious Bias training program, including a deep dive for a broad set of executives across

IRI globally. Our program helps individuals examine how the decisions we make are based on our own experiences, upbringings, set of biases, etc., influencing whether we realize it or not, our talent decisions. The quicker we individually and collectively recognize these biases and work to minimize their influence, the better we will be at making the right decisions for each employee, our teams, and the business.

And of course, our work goes well beyond our employees too. A critical anchor point in our approach is to take the same proven technology, analytics and talent expertise we apply to prominent global consumer goods and retail companies every day and bring it to minority-owned businesses in their communities. By providing similar services at scale to those businesses, we can help them connect the dots across the industry, accelerate their path forward to success, and positively impact their communities. We are committed to this work and will continue to reflect both on the "what we do and how we do it" to support our local communities and businesses.

KEY TENETS

TO THE DIVERSITY, EQUITY, AND INCLUSION PHILOSOPHY AT IRI

WE BELIEVE in the undeniable strength that diverse people, culture, thought and skill bring to our business, our clients, our people, and our communities

WE ARE COMMITTED to nurturing a dynamic culture that embraces and celebrates openness, collaboration, creativity, equity, inclusivity, and growth for all

OUR BELIEFS ARE ROOTED in the diversity of heritage, origin, orientation, perspective, experience, and expertise

WE ARE DEDICATED to using our unique position, assets, and relationships to support diverse and minority-led businesses to strengthen our communities

HOW

IRI SUPPORTS DIVERSITY, EQUITY, AND INCLUSION THROUGHOUT THE EMPLOYEE LIFECYCLE

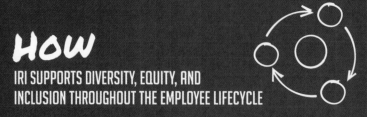

IRI looks at critical moments throughout the employee experience to capture a full understanding of progress. We look at all the moments that matter for an employee, ranging from the candidate experience to how we engage each employee to create an inclusive culture. We also consider key transition details so leaders have insight into why employees choose alternatives to our organization. The key areas and a sample of measures we look at include:

RECRUIT:
Are we building the right makeup of employees we hire, both for early career and more experienced roles?

ENGAGE:
Is our total workforce engaged in our diversity, equity, and inclusion efforts?

GROW:
What are our promotion rates at all levels, and are we growing toward more employee awareness, understanding, and enhanced skills?

TRANSITION:
What are our turnover rates and our scores specifically related to a diverse and inclusive workforce environment on exit surveys?

So, how does the fact that you partner with very diverse organizations make it even more important for you to build a more diverse workforce?

A The global companies we serve sell their products to a broad set of consumers—a blend of diversity, backgrounds, and experiences. For us to provide the greatest level of expertise, understanding, thought, and business strategies that deliver impact, we must strive to reflect a similar profile of diversity. Additionally, to maximize our partnerships with clients, having a shared set of values is a critical success factor. Before all the data, insights, and analytics are delivered, a common purpose around teaming, collaboration, communication, and experiences are established—rapidly pushing the partnership forward with greater success.

I'm curious about the listening sessions you've had with employees over the last year. What are some of the discussions like inside IRI around your diversity, equity, and inclusion goals?

A Discussion threads are as varied and diverse as you can imagine, driven by the experiences and vantage points each participant brings to the conversation.

Discussions ranged in content and intensity—focusing on topics like recruiting, metrics and business results, news, and the impacts on each of us personally and collectively, and what IRI is going to do to progress.

One thread throughout the discussions that is resoundingly clear to all of us is the notion that building an inclusive and diverse workforce enabling every unique individual to have an "exceptional experience" is simply the right thing to do.

I believe we can't progress towards strengthening diversity, equity and inclusion without first focusing on establishing the following: *Creating an environment where people are really engaged and excited to come to work, where relationships exist more deeply than the day-to-day tasks, and building an environment where each individual's work contributes to answering their "personal why."*

What are some of the other big principles to consider when it comes to advancing diversity and inclusion?

A First principle to align to is that there is no "magical" panacea. There won't be a moment where we jam the flag in the sand and claim victory. This is an ongoing journey with many stops along the way that requires focus, energy, and consistency for improvement versus having a conclusive destination. It starts and persists with listening and learning. There's a heck of a lot of people inside and outside this organization who have different views, depth on the subject, or ideas, which is great. And as we go down this "path for progress," we must continue to vet all ideas, actively pull in our teammates to be part of the journey, and empower our colleagues to contribute to the progress we desire directly. This is NOT an "I" thing or a leadership team accountability directive— this is a "we" thing and an effort that requires a collective set of people to fly in the same direction.

Taking a one-size-fits-all approach is also not the answer. Rolling out a DEI Toolkit and sending out some messaging or talking points for me does not equate to an impactful, personalized, and comprehensive path for progress. DEI is an "active sport" that requires daily engagement and practice. Yes, there are different tactics that we can apply across the organization, like Unconscious Bias training or a refreshed candidate selection process. But we must blend those efforts with individualized elements—enabling each employee in partnership with their leaders/teams to create a unique experience that's personal, helps them grow, and allows them to be a part of something that's important to them.

THIS IS A 'WE' THING

Building on this notion of personalization is similar to consumers and how retailers strive to make shopping a more personal experience that meets their unique consumers' preferences. When we buy something from a store, that store's goal is to understand your buying patterns better and more intimately interact

THIS IS A VERY
PERSONAL TOPIC

with you in the store and when you're at home to build better experiences for you. They connect with you about products and promotions that are personal to you. That makes your experience more comfortable, unique, and tailored to your needs.

Similarly, we have to shape our inclusion and engagement efforts based on the organization's personalities and how it fits with the established set of core values and culture. This is a very personal topic. If you don't make it personal, showing empathy and consideration for each person's feelings, opinions, and stories, your likelihood of having a deep and meaningful connection and momentum decreases, landing you with results that have depth only at the surface and last for a short period.

That's a good point about being genuinely committed to this work. On a related note, what do you say to employees who may be skeptical about this or to people who think it may impact them adversely?

A I just believe that regardless of race, gender, or any other characteristic you may represent, the way you add the most value to any team is figuring out how you can differentiate yourself and offer talents and contributions that are unique. If you can act upon those unique talents, you will always drive value and outcomes for the organization.

When I look at what many organizations are trying to achieve at the end of the day, I see overall engagement as a big part of it. While that sounds great on paper, it's probably hard for a lot of organizations to accomplish in a time of crisis, when there are so many demands on the business and so many things being asked of employees.

A When I was a kid, I loved reading the *Choose Your Own Adventure* books. When you got to page five, you could choose where to take the story—either jump on the spaceship and head to a new planet or keep your spacesuit on and continue to explore. Critical to the book and the reader was the idea that we had choices. Like childhood books, people leadership, talent development, and employee engagement tend to work the same way. It's all about the perspective you take, the choices you make, and playing out the outcomes.

For example, when I have a set of leaders resistant to embracing new engagement efforts or making the investment to have a career discussion, my response might be "Let's play out the *Choose Your Own Adventure* storyline related to your team." I proceed to walk them through two options. Option A is an employee comes to you as a high performer and says, "I want to do community service as part of an ERG

CHOOSE YOUR OWN ADVENTURE

PEOPLE
LEADERSHIP

effort next week." Too often, the leader responds with, "We've got all these client deliverables now. Next week isn't good. Maybe next time." The employee goes back and is disappointed or defeated but still willing to accept the "no" for one time. But if they come back to you a month later and say, "I want to take this training course next month to build my skills, and it requires me to be away and focused for two days," and you say "no" again, then you've just permanently disengaged that person.

Let us then play out the next set of outcomes because of that simple "no"—they decide to leave the firm and find a different job where they can engage in a variety of personalized experiences important to them. They also post on social media channels their lack of opportunity to grow and contribute in different areas along with sharing their experience with their network. You now explain to the client why your high performer left the team. You then spend a few months recruiting candidates, selecting a new teammate, onboarding and training them up. Six months later, that new employee is finally up to speed, but only after significant investments in your time and likely others on the team filling in for the vacancy.

Option B is that you look at your teammate and say, "I absolutely think you should join next week's community service event or attend the training session as it sounds really important to you. So, let's figure out a plan for how you do those things and complete your work as well." With that, you empower that employee. You massively increase engagement with that individual and likely get higher performance from them in the future and don't spend months rebuilding the team.

"YOU EMPOWER THAT EMPLOYEE

When you frame up the *Choose Your Own Adventure* engagement choice, the answer seems pretty obvious. Yet, the options so many managers intuitively take are the ones exclusively focused on the short term needs of the business or require a bit more work to identify a workable plan. **The bottom line is if you want to drive deeper engagement, learn to listen better, build a plan that's important and personal to your employees, and partner with them to make it happen.**

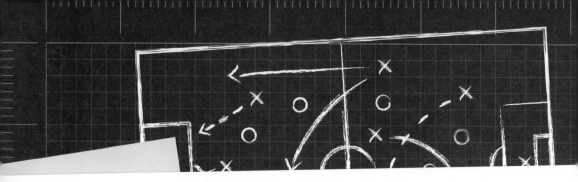

As you think about trying to make real progress on inclusion and diversity, what still keeps you up at night?

A To ensure this work doesn't become the flavor of the day. How do we keep the energy and passion at the top of the list—as a top priority individually and collectively? How does the DEI journey at our company and others stay at equal footing and importance as the firm's other strategic priorities? Firmly aligning with boards and leadership teams, building this priority into performance measures, consistently communicating progress and updates, and consistently empowering employees to participate and have their voices heard—those are examples of how these efforts sustain themselves and build better, stronger, healthier businesses.

It's clear that you're personally passionate about building a more diverse and inclusive workforce. Is there a personal experience you've had that helped shape your views?

A Sports has played an enormous role in my life; I've been playing soccer since I was four years old. Over time, I've reflected more on the diversity required for a winning team. If you think about the highest performing teams, you're not seeing coaches putting all the same types of skill sets on the field at once. The soccer team positions—goalie, defense, midfield, forwards—each requires a real diversity of experience, skillset, and capabilities. When coaches work to create that winning dynamic, they know that diverse energy, effective communication, and varied abilities build great teams and make winning championships possible.

So why would we not think that way within a business setting? Assembling a team with similar experiences, expertise, or skills may produce a win or two but won't be a sustainable winning formula to produce business "championships" and engage talent in the long term. For me, winning sports teams are easily one of the best examples of great diversity and what inclusion gets you.

INCLUSION + DIVERSITY =
WINNING FORMULA

Evan Swidler is the Chief People Officer for IRI, leading global human resources, talent engagement, and organizational change efforts. Before joining IRI, Swidler was Chief Human Resources Officer for ATI Physical Therapy. He also held various senior executive roles for The Nielsen Company and served as a commercial leader in Accenture's Management Consulting practice.

You have a different perspective as the leader of a company that is 100 percent employee-owned. Can you share how being employee-owned shapes the way you think about leadership in a time of crisis or change?

A Amsted has been employee-owned since 1985, and owned 100 percent by its employee stock ownership plan, or ESOP, since 1998. All of our businesses are market leaders, and over the last 20 years we've seen share price growth close to 20 percent on an annualized basis. One of the best parts of that growth is seeing our employees directly benefit from it, in significant ways. Thousands of our employees have retired very secure financially—and that includes a lot of people doing tough jobs on the foundry or shop floor.

Because we're not answering to public shareholders every quarter, we also benefit from taking a more long-term approach to business, which is of particular help in a time of crisis or challenge. We don't have to make short-term decisions just to please analysts. As we are investing in innovation and new technologies, this is crucial; we can plan. Our long-term view is also very important because we have cyclical businesses—we will always have ups and downs, and we can adjust to that, while always working to see that the ups are higher and the lows are not as low.

Now to be clear—we have had to right-size our businesses in the face of dramatically reduced demand. However, our employees understand that we are in cyclical businesses, that the markets will come back, and that taking some hard actions now is good for our employee owners in the long term. As a result, I think we've been able to limit the pandemic-induced stress in our organization. Things have been relatively calm. We have a culture here anyway that thrives on fixing problems so for many of us, this has all been another important problem to fix. All of that confidence from our people helps, and I simply try to mirror the confidence of our people and not show any signs of panic. And, I have to say it's been a great advantage to have lived through the great recession just 10 to 12 years ago, too.

"IN THE MIDST OF A STORM, BE A CALM AND CONFIDENT VOICE

.ıll 🛜   100% 🔋

How have you communicated about your experience during the 2008 recession to help calm the nerves?

A One thing I've done a lot is walking people through the recession and what happened to our share price and our businesses then, and how a couple of years after that, we had come all the way back and grown far beyond our previous highs. And I think that was very calming for people to understand. This strategy of showing how we've been here before, we've made it through and come out the other side, has been very effective. It reminds people that while this may look different and feel different, there's still so much that's similar that we can get right.

What challenges go along with being employee-owned that may have made the pandemic tougher to manage for you?

A Yes, there are naturally two sides to the equation when it comes to employee ownership. Because our employees have wealth tied up in our shares, when you suddenly take hits from closing a plant for two months or a significant drop in share price, now you've got an employee workforce that's dealing not only with the pandemic, but their future wealth that has been cut. While you could say that would make it more difficult in some ways, I'm glad to say that I haven't seen that, and I think that goes back to the historical success we've had. We are a cyclical company and we have people who are mature about that. They understand that also means that they'll get granted shares at that lower price, which they think will ultimately work to their advantage too. So, from a pure financial standpoint, even challenging financial hits can be viewed as an opportunity.

Are there new things you're doing to help set a positive tone, despite the challenges?

A The fact that we're all owners together is a point I emphasize. In fact, that's the overall leadership tone I always try to set—that I'm just a fellow owner with you. It's that whole, all-hands-on-deck kind of attitude that helps. We also convey this approach through our leadership training. I make the point repeatedly that leadership is not about Steve Smith. Instead, we want leadership to be a core trait for all our employees. We've spent a lot of time talking about leadership and what makes a leader, and our attitude about what leadership is, that it's not pounding on the table, but working to be the rock at the center. And while we have a lot of different personalities among our leadership team itself, that characteristic runs through most of our leaders. Another big part of leadership here is trustworthiness. If you're not trustworthy, and don't lead with integrity, you're not going to rise to the highest levels of leadership at Amsted.

It sounds like you've worked a lot on building a culture that values everyone and their unique perspectives.

A Being owned by employees definitely helps shape our values, and it naturally results in a shared DNA across our businesses and geographies. The structure of our ESOP and other benefits means that we all benefit from the success of every business—so helping another business to grow and learn benefits us all. At the core of our business is a culture of integrity, creativity, authenticity, energy and candor. Our strength is in how we work with one another with a common purpose—and as some of our employees phrase it, interact on the basis of love, dignity and respect.

What are some of the other benefits of employee ownership that help you navigate change from a position of strength?

A With our growth and ESOP model, our employees benefit in ways that they can't in other organizations or industries. A few years ago after we announced a very positive quarterly earnings report and share price increase, a supervisor walked out on the floor and saw this guy working on a machine—covered in grease—but just beaming. The supervisor asked why, and the guy said, "I'm really happy today. Today, I am a millionaire." He had done the math and knew his accounts. That's true of thousands of employees. I'm proud that we work in a company with businesses where everyone benefits—and where we continue to grow in smaller communities where these employees can live well, raise their families and retire confidently. The ESOP model and Amsted are enabling the American Dream for our employees. At a time when there is a lot of focus on wealth inequality, our structure is one that spreads the wealth we all earn together more broadly, as we share not only in the fruits of our labor, but share in building our capital value as well.

The ESOP structure is a uniquely U.S. structure—how does this work in a global company like Amsted?

A You are right, at this point we are able to directly extend the benefit of ownership to our U.S. employees. We always look for ways that we could extend it more broadly, but at this point the tax and other laws of other countries in which we operate make that very difficult. We do take steps, however, to see that leaders around the world participate in a meaningful way in our growth. Also, our strength as an ESOP company has enabled us to grow significantly in global markets, producing Amsted jobs and lives of dignity for thousands around the globe. And our operations in all those countries still carry all the Amsted values inherent in our employee ownership culture—some of that same love, dignity and respect.

Within this culture, how exactly does a leader make his or her mark?

A The future for Amsted is about each of us stepping forward and raising his or her hand. Our leaders try to reinforce this message all the time, this idea that our future is in the hands of all of us, owning our results and always looking for what comes "next" in whatever we do. My primary legacy at Amsted will be the people and culture I leave behind. I am committed to ensuring we have the next level of leaders ready to take Amsted to new levels of prosperity through innovation and ownership.

In times of crisis and uncertainty, what else do you think plays a big role in effective leadership?

A I find my background as an attorney helps me a lot in my role as a CEO. I've always felt that knowledge is power and that's especially evident in the field of corporate law. While I don't ever want to fall into "analysis paralysis" because you have to be able to make decisions at the end of the day, I believe that understanding the key elements of a situation is what will always help me make the best decisions.

And that comes down to better conversations, better questions, and better listening. I feel like my work as a lawyer really honed this mindset and informed my style as a leader. I like to apply the art of cross-examination—asking questions and listening—so I can learn. Listening in my mind is infinitely more important than talking and can reveal answers we never expected. It's important to take in all the information, observe, and consider the facts to avoid jumping to conclusions.

CONSIDER THE FACTS

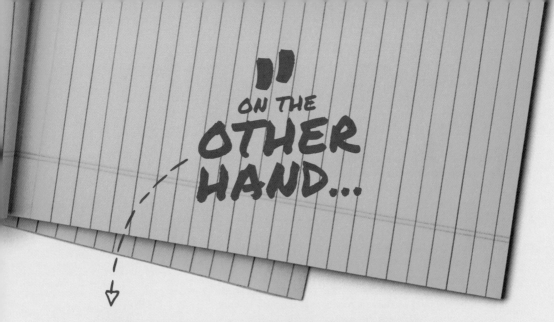

"ON THE OTHER HAND...

...while good input is important, there comes a time as a leader when you have to trust your gut.

I think back to the time four years ago when Amsted faced a significant transition after the unexpected passing of my predecessor, Bob Reum, after 16 years of incredibly effective leadership. Our Board had been doing good work on succession, but Bob's death was sudden and unexpected, and there wasn't a clear path to succession. I was originally asked to serve as interim CEO of Amsted while they conducted an outside search.

I was happy to help in that capacity, but when I looked at this company at that moment in time, it was clear to me that an internal candidate who understood the strength of Amsted's employee culture would best capitalize on that strength. I am not generally a self-promoter, but I told the Board they didn't need to search outside Amsted and I didn't want the role to be interim…and here we are. From that I learned that when something strikes you as right, don't hesitate—commit to it. I'm all about gathering information and making an informed decision, but there will be times when the answer becomes apparent to you and you know that it is the right time to make a move. It is important to listen to that voice.

I know your faith means a lot to you as well. Have you leaned on faith while leading through the pandemic?

A I've seen how faith can help many people through challenging times in their lives. I shared a bit of this personal view with all of our employees through a series of letters and videos over the last several months. In one video, I described how my wife, Linda, and I sat at our kitchen table and watched our church's service on my laptop because we couldn't attend personally due to the pandemic. Our pastor and music conductor were speaking and singing with the empty pews behind them, where we normally would be sitting. On the one hand, it was sad, in that the empty pews reminded us how much we missed being in fellowship with our fellow parishioners. But at the same time, it was a profound and comforting reminder that we are all part of something that transcends even this crisis, and that this too shall pass. The message I tried to share through that video was my confidence in our Amsted family, and my belief that we, too, will make it through the current challenges and come out on the other side, stronger for it, with our spirit of ownership and innovation reinvigorated.

THIS TOO SHALL PASS

Stephen Smith is Chairman, President and Chief Executive Officer at Amsted Industries. Prior to joining Amsted, Steve was general counsel and President of Shared Services Operations in North America of GKN plc, a FTSE-traded UK diversified engineering company; and from 1991 to 1999 was Vice President, Secretary and General Counsel of The Interlake Corporation, an NYSE-traded diversified manufacturing company. Steve began his legal career in 1982 at the Chicago law firm of Hopkins & Sutter (since merged into Foley & Lardner), where he was a Corporate Partner and Chairman of the Corporate Transactions Group.

CHAPTER 2

LEAD YOURSELF
FIRST

Practical knowledge and time-saving
tips we've learned from more than
20 years of **thought**partnership
with clients—along with lessons from
Change Makers who describe what
exceptional leadership looks like.

WE HEAR THIS CONCEPT WHEN WE'RE ABOUT TO TAKE OFF ON A PLANE:

In case of an emergency, put your own oxygen mask on first before helping children or others.

Leaders need to lead with this same mentality. Addressing your key needs first lets you be more available to those counting on you, whether that's your direct reports, your peers, or others across the organization who need help. Taking care of **YOU** at a basic level also helps you avoid taking out your stress or frustration on others.

- ✓ GET ENOUGH REST
- ✓ EAT WELL
- ✓ GET FRESH AIR AND EXERCISE
- ✓ SELF-REFLECT MORE

THIS IS WHERE SELF-AWARENESS COMES INTO PLAY

Recognize that your emotions may go up and down during an hour, during the day, or during the week, even during one conversation. Just because we're a leader doesn't mean we're immune from the same range of emotions and feelings our teams are going through. The watchword here is "gentle." How might you be as gentle with yourself as you aspire to be with others? Self-compassion is important because it opens up the capacity for compassion for others.

RECOGNIZE WHEN IT'S TIME TO DELAY PERSONAL COMMUNICATION

When you're bothered or feeling low, remember that it's very difficult to communicate, not to mention communicate with heart. You might be irritable, want to blame someone, feel angry or feel like you're worrying excessively. All those feelings are okay, natural in many cases, and give you useful information about how you're doing. Here's the key: This is just not the ideal time to be communicating.

HEAD, HEART & GUTS LEADERSHIP

01

Hillrom, a global medical device manufacturer where I serve as Advisor to the CEO, has been dealing with the impact of the pandemic since the early days of its spread, starting in China. With operations in hard-hit areas, we were concerned with the health and safety of our employees and our ability to continue serving customers, who needed us more than ever. By early March 2020, we had transitioned nearly all of our office-based team members, thousands of people globally, to remote work. The stress for those still going to manufacturing plants and into hospitals every day, as well as on those now juggling jobs and family-care duties at home as schools and day care centers shut down, was (and remains) significant.

We recognized that mental health, an issue very dear to me personally, was something we needed to address directly, and for which we needed to create a safe space internally. The subject of mental health is a sensitive one that is important all the time, and especially during a prolonged crisis such as the COVID-19 pandemic. Feelings of anxiety or worry, sadness or depression are normal, and each one of us handled the pandemic, and handles any difficult situation, in highly individual ways. How we manage what we are feeling is important for ourselves and our families, and recognizing our mental-health needs is the very first step to ensure that we take proper care of ourselves not only physically but emotionally and mentally as well.

Our team decided upon a two-pronged approach. I recorded a short video message addressing the importance of watching for signs of stress, strain, anxiety and depression. We distributed that video in late March 2020 along with a written message that included Employee Assistance Programs (EAP), telehealth, and government-provided mental health resources for our locations around the world. We also invited employees to share with us, for publication, their own coping mechanisms (at right).

The response was overwhelming! I received dozens of messages from colleagues around the world. The combination of a senior leader discussing mental health so openly, and employees making their own contributions to the dialogue, created the space we needed to ensure our employees knew we cared for their mental health as much as their physical health.

As the opening of this chapter captured, remember what you hear from flight attendants before take-off: "Take care of yourself before helping others." Doing so ensures you will have the mental and physical abilities needed to take care of others. The principle for our Hillrom team is the same—we are likely to be more effective supporting our colleagues or our families at home if we first are able to take care of ourselves.

Following are just some of the mental health coping mechanisms submitted by Hillrom employees:

- I walk with my wife in the fields around my house at the end of the day, when the sun is setting. I was never so aware and appreciative of the beautiful nature right where I live.

- Each morning, I choose a different meditation. I am finding this to be very helpful, especially during these challenging times.

- Regular informal contact with colleagues helps keeping spirits up and the team together, we meet every day for a virtual coffee break.

THE CHANGE MAKERS

Ken Meyers is currently Advisor to the CEO for Hillrom, a leading global medical technology company. Meyers had previously served as Senior Vice President and Chief Human Resources Officer for Hillrom and has three decades of senior leadership, Board of Directors, HR and operations experience. Before joining Hillrom, Meyers served as the SVP/CHRO of Hospira.

02

LISTENING WITH GRATITUDE, LETTING YOUR AUTHENTIC SELF SHINE THROUGH

What I have observed and learned is that people want to know that you're human; they want you to strip away the political pretense and show some vulnerability. We often try to hide our vulnerabilities at work. Instead, we need to let our authentic selves shine through. There is, of course, a very important balance to strike, because as a leader, we still need to instill confidence while being ourselves. When you get into the flow of that, it feels really good and it creates an environment that is naturally more open. An open, trusting environment lets diverse voices rise. When people

see leaders being themselves and showing some vulnerability, they trust that they can also be themselves and feel safe in expressing their opinions and ideas. At the most basic level, it's just leading by example, that old leadership cliché. When you've made this kind of human connection, you can ask the workforce what they think, how they're feeling, and they'll respond more honestly. When you ask, it's important to listen with gratitude.

To me, this means listening without judgment and showing appreciation for the trust the person has extended to you in sharing their feelings and insights. Listening with gratitude shows respect for the individual and leaves the open space for dialogue and conversation.

As a leader, this concept can be challenging; we are accustomed to having "all" the answers, to responding quickly. Leaders need to break this paradigm for themselves and stay "in listen-only mode" more often. Likewise, leaders need to develop a more robust ability to move into uncomfortable places, even feel a sense of nervousness. Assumptions need to be left at the door so that new perspectives can actually be considered.

It isn't an easy thing to do, but this kind of listening becomes easier with practice. The power of this kind of listening experience can't be overstated. When people share something that is very personal and when they help you recognize where they're coming from, it's something to be thankful for and something that we can grow from.

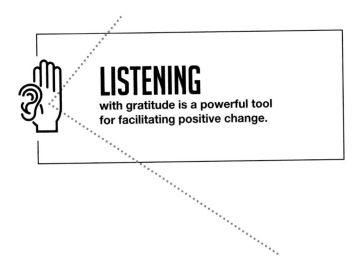

LISTENING
with gratitude is a powerful tool for facilitating positive change.

Renae Chorzempa is the former Executive Vice President and Chief HR Officer for InnerWorkings. She was responsible for helping the company reach its fullest organizational potential by building and growing its talent capabilities.

SELF-CARE FOR LEADERS

The concept of regularly setting aside time for personal needs can seem frivolous or weak to many leaders today. Some just resign themselves to sacrificing personal time for the good of the business. Or, they may recognize the value of some down time, yet still quickly fall into a crisis mode mentality, jumping from one "fire drill" to the next, barely taking the time to breathe. The toll this takes on the leader's personal well-being and that of the organization may not be obvious or intuitive. In fact, our culture supports being busy and working long hours as a hallmark of great leadership. Yet research demonstrates that while hard work is necessary for success, it should not come at the expense of addressing basic human needs for self-reflection and stress reduction. Ultimately, failing to self-care has its own pitfalls, and they quickly add up.

Here are 5 key benefits[1] of self-care for leaders:

1. Reduces your stress level, improves your health

As many leaders can attest, not all stress is bad. When managed well, natural stress can stimulate leaders into positive action or a high-alert status, often described as the "fight-or-flight response." The problem comes when stress is chronic and not managed, leading to leaders operating in a constant state of high alert and high anxiety. This has serious impacts on a leader's nervous system, which can equate to more health problems, weakened immune systems (particularly not helpful during a pandemic) and poor mental health. Psychologists have long chronicled the many long-term impacts of stress on mental and physical health. According to the National Institute of Mental Health, continued strain on your body from stress contributes to a range of critical health problems, including heart disease, high blood pressure, diabetes and other illnesses, such as depression and anxiety.

[1]National Institute of Mental Health, "5 Things You Should Know About Stress," 2019

EFFECTS OF STRESS ON YOUR BODY[2]

HEADACHES
Stress can trigger and intensify

DEPRESSION
Chronic stress can wear
you down emotionally

WEAKENED IMMUNE SYSTEM
Long-term stress weakens your defense,
leaving you more vulnerable to infections

HEARTBURN
Stress increases production of stomach acid

HIGH BLOOD PRESSURE
Stress hormones tighten
blood vessels

MUSCLE TENSION
Stress can lead to tension-related
backaches and pains

[2]Healthline, "The Effects of Stress on Your Body," 2017

2. Sets a positive tone from the top

Leaders operating under a constant vibe of stress and anxiety often set off a ripple effect on their teams. According to a recent study from workforce consulting firm Life Meets Work, only 11 percent of employees with stressed leaders felt highly engaged at work. Further, only 7 percent of employees believed that their stressed leaders effectively led their teams. "A leader's inability to manage stress ripples through the entire organization in a negative way," reported Kenneth Matos, psychologist and Vice President of Research for Life Meets Work. By contrast, leaders who take the time to manage their stress and operate from a calm and confident approach set a positive tone that has a powerful impact on the entire team. The psychologist Barbara Fredrickson finds that generating more positive emotions also enhances people's ability to think creatively and develop innovative ideas or solutions.

HOW LEADER STRESS IMPACTS EMPLOYEES

Life Meets Work, a workforce consulting firm, surveyed U.S. employees on their leader's ability to handle stress and how that leader's approach impacted their own feelings about work. They found:

ONLY **7%**
of employees believe stressed leaders effectively lead their teams

11% ONLY
of employees with stressed leaders are highly engaged at work

3. Enables personal improvement

As any successful leader knows, if you're not learning, you're not growing. One of the best ways to learn is to take the time to self-reflect. Some key questions to ask yourself include: Am I bringing my best self to work every day? What am I doing well? What could I be doing better? If I was really honest with myself, what would I say is the single biggest flaw in my leadership today? Many leaders miss just how important this kind of exercise can be. According to a study reported in *Harvard Business Review*, people who spent 15 minutes at the end of the day reflecting on lessons learned performed 23 percent better after 10 days than those who did not reflect.

4. Makes you more energetic

Just like high-performance athletes who understand the necessity for rest and recovery time, leaders who take care of themselves tend to perform better. Self-care activities are naturally quite individual to the leader, but could include all forms of exercise, breathing exercises, meditation, journaling, regular meals with friends, massages or power naps. The key is to avoid the short-term "comfort" habits that can lead to their own drains on energy over time, including excessive drinking or eating. And an extra word on exercise. Whatever your choice of exercise, keep in mind that it's doubly beneficial, helping to reduce stress and boost energy. This is because the physical activity generates neurochemicals that help with focus and attention. Research also suggests that more time outside—through rigorous exercise or leisurely walks—can improve mood, cognition and general health.

5. Produces better overall results for your organization

As we all know, people don't leave organizations; they leave bad bosses. If your stress levels get out of control, you're inviting more of your employees to run for the exit signs. Research bears this out: According to *Gallup's State of the American Manager Report*, managers account for at least 70 percent of the variance in employee engagement scores. Gallup found that unhappy, unhealthy employees affect their organizations in a myriad of ways, including absenteeism, performance, customer ratings, quality and profit.

GROWING EMPLOYEE STRESS
Study demonstrates depth of stress

Experts in the field have now confirmed our suspicions. For more than a decade, the American Psychological Association (APA) has conducted a comprehensive survey in conjunction with Harris Polls of the sources and intensity of stress that people are experiencing. In releasing the 2020 survey, the APA noted, "We are facing a national mental health crisis that could yield serious health and social consequences for years to come." According to the survey:

19%

SAY THEIR MENTAL HEALTH IS WORSE THAN LAST YEAR

60%

SAY THE NUMBER OF ISSUES AMERICA CURRENTLY FACES IS OVERWHELMING

49%

REPORT THEIR BEHAVIOR HAS BEEN NEGATIVELY AFFECTED BY STRESS: INCREASED TENSION IN THEIR BODIES (21%), "SNAPPING" OR GETTING ANGRY VERY QUICKLY (20%), UNEXPECTED MOOD SWINGS (20%), OR SCREAMING OR YELLING AT A LOVED ONE (17%)

2 IN 3 64%
ADULTS

**SAY MONEY IS A SIGNIFICANT
SOURCE OF STRESS**

77%

**OF ADULTS SAY
THE FUTURE OF
OUR NATION IS
A SOURCE OF
STRESS, UP FROM
66% IN 2019**

Employers can help <u>reduce</u> employee stress levels

The APA's detailed findings are broadly based and document information from many demographics including Gen Z, younger students and low-income individuals. According to the APA, here's what you can do: Provide clear communication to employees and supervisors in three main areas—expectations, support resources and new policies that respond directly to impacts created by the pandemic and other stressors. This will reduce uncertainty at work, which is a major contributor to employee stress.

03

FOLLOW THE FOUR Vs

 VULNERABLE

More and more, I've realized the value of showing some vulnerability—some humanness—as a leader. This was a fairly significant paradigm shift for me, as I suspect it might be for many leaders. We can feel like we are supposed to have all the answers. Yet, by showing your own vulnerability, you give people the freedom to let their own guard down too. Through that, you discover more common ground.

When I was in Phoenix, I took the risk to open up a discussion about the racial unrest and violence in our community. During the discussion, I mentioned that I didn't know what I could do personally to help. Members of my team challenged me and offered suggestions for what I could do. I appreciated that because it led to a healthy conversation about everyone's personal responsibility to help heal the racial divides in our cities. This reinforced the idea that what might initially seem like a tough discussion can actually create an open dialogue that fosters new perspectives and new potential solutions.

2 VORACIOUS

Be voracious in your information gathering. No matter the challenge you face, it's important to talk to your peers in the company to understand how they are managing things, and also from top leaders to learn what the company is thinking and considering. Ideally, you're part of these conversations anyway so it's a natural discussion process. Further, get the pulse of the outside community from social media and news outlets because that's what your employees are looking at too. All of this helps you prepare for the team's questions and concerns.

3 VOCAL

During a crisis, it is more important than ever to communicate constantly. Share what you know, when you know it, even if the answer is "I don't know right now." And make sure you let your leadership know how your team is feeling and what they're doing as well. Communication should be two-way, up and down the chain, so your team's voices are always heard.

4 VISIBLE

Be visible to your team. Make it clear that you are available and check in more frequently than usual, especially with those who aren't direct reports as you likely wouldn't see them as much. During the pandemic, I called each of my team members to just check in. I made the point that I wasn't calling about business matters, just to see how they were coping.

I also took the time to share my appreciation for all they were doing for the business. When a leader is willing to share their personal truths and break down barriers, employees will do the same. Perhaps most significantly, with a more caring, humanizing culture, people work harder, demonstrate more creativity and are more engaged.

Joe Ricciardi is Executive Director of Internal Communications for The Villages, a Florida retirement community. Prior to that role, he served as Director of Employee Communications for Arizona Public Service, the largest electric utility company in Arizona.

HOW SOLITUDE CAN MAKE YOU A BETTER LEADER

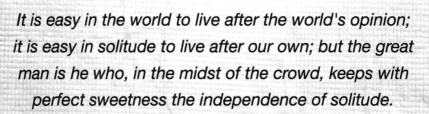

It is easy in the world to live after the world's opinion; it is easy in solitude to live after our own; but the great man is he who, in the midst of the crowd, keeps with perfect sweetness the independence of solitude.

- RALPH WALDO EMERSON

The renowned poet Ralph Waldo Emerson couldn't have said it better: Solitude has great power. That's especially true for anyone who wants to be a standout leader, making the kind of wise and well-considered decisions that move organizations to new heights. Yet achieving solitude is easier said than done for today's leaders, who are constantly bombarded with noise of all kinds—meetings, conference calls, social media, news reports, and mounds of email.

Confronting that noise from stakeholders big and small, leaders may be tempted to ignore the need for solitude. Speed of decision making becomes the priority, yet often at the price of innovation and creativity. If you're frenetically putting out fires or checking the boxes, your leadership is probably only reflecting conventional wisdom. You're not fostering the kind of breakthrough innovations to help your organization soar past the competition, lead and win.

In the book, *Lead Yourself First*, authors Raymond Kethledge and Michael S. Erwin describe the critical relationship between solitude and great leadership. The authors share how many exceptional leaders have used solitude to make better decisions, including historical figures such as Martin Luther King Jr., Abraham Lincoln and Dwight Eisenhower, as well as prominent figures in business today. The leaders' moments of solitude come in all different forms—gardening, hiking, running, fly fishing, meditation, journaling, etc.—whatever helped them discover calm and perspective.

Kethledge, a prominent federal court judge, explained in an interview with a legal journal why the book was personally so important to research and write, and the message he hoped to send leaders today: "Solitude has been important to all kinds of leaders, and we are losing solitude today—without realizing it, and without making a conscious choice. What we're trying to say in *Lead Yourself First* is this: Not only do you have permission to seek solitude, but you have a duty. If you lead people, you have a duty to seek solitude so that you can lead them effectively and ethically."

Whatever your method of choice, consider opportunities for solitude as one of the greatest gifts you can give your organization today.

04

BUILD YOUR TEAM RELATIONSHIPS AND MODEL THE CHANGE YOU WANT TO SEE

When I reflect on leading in times of change, several lessons come to mind. First is the importance of building strong, internal relationships early on during change. This sounds obvious, but all changes have cheerleaders and detractors and it is equally important to engage both groups in the change process so everyone—especially the detractors—feel they have a voice and are involved in making the change.

At Amazon, we are constantly growing and evolving so it's critical to take a step back and think about change strategically versus just trying to "convince" employees of the value. When leaders take the time to be more strategic, they can build more acceptance within the organization and ensure long-term success. Be sure to

also review change rollout progress with your key internal audiences as a change is rolled out and evolves. That effort builds trust and helps teams work together more closely on future changes.

One of the most important audiences often overlooked during change is the team actually managing the change itself. It is often easy to get busy and focus solely on project execution and lose sight of the value of the team's daily work. I try to challenge myself and my team to say, "What's the true value of this project? How are we actually improving the employee experience with this tool, process, or communication?" Taking a step back for this assessment increases the quality of execution and helps team members stay focused and excited about how their work contributes to the employee experience. The COVID-19 pandemic forced many companies and leaders to think more about the human side of managing employees. For me, it serves as a critical reminder that we need to continually find ways to work with individual employees to support their personal needs and help them be more productive.

For instance, I had team members who were struggling to balance work and care for young kids at home during the pandemic. We rescheduled calls and team meeting times to give them more flexibility to balance childcare responsibilities. I feel strongly that we should equip managers to model this type of flexibility, even outside times of change. For example, I try to uphold a "policy" for myself of no meetings/conference calls on Fridays whenever possible. It allows me uninterrupted time to reflect, regroup and focus on the big picture, and I encourage my team to do the same for themselves.

Yes, as an organization we still need policies and processes, but we need to empower managers to be flexible and build in creative approaches to help employees be successful and drive valuable work. Seeing an employee as a whole person goes a long way to creating stronger organizational commitment and loyalty.

THE
CHANGE
MAKERS

Michele Williams is a Senior Program Manager at Amazon. She leads teams in employee relations and has also been a leader in global communications.

❝ HOW ARE WE ACTUALLY *IMPROVING* THE EMPLOYEE EXPERIENCE WITH THIS...

TOOL / PROCESS / COMMUNICATION?

05

RECOGNIZING THE IMPORTANCE OF PERSONAL CONNECTIONS AND KNOWING WHEN IT'S TIME TO SHIFT YOUR LEADERSHIP STYLE

I am a person who thrives on building a personal connection with people and when I was in a plant, it was normal for me to walk around engaging in conversations with the workforce. Through the years, I have worked to build strong relationships with employees by getting to know people as individuals. Likewise, getting regular feedback has been an important part of my style. When you are working together day to day, I think all of this is more easily done. One of my lessons learned is that building these relationships remains even more essential in a virtual landscape. Doing so is entirely possible, but it takes more effort to continue to make this leadership style happen. So, I have made a shift, and make it a point to check in at the beginning of calls/online meetings with more personal interactions: "How are you doing? How is your family doing? How was your weekend?" Sounds simple, but we are accustomed to focusing so much on the business and performance that we overlook that we are experiencing a very different environment, as there is uncertainty around when in-person meetings will resume. On the business side, I have always also asked many questions and made a point of trying to be a good listener; I have redoubled my efforts in this regard.

In addition, I make myself even more available to my direct reports with one-on-one sessions and they can be at times when it is most convenient for that person. Because conventional hours may not be feasible as many are balancing more virtual meetings along with having family members home, too. When group or individual calls are finished, I often send a follow-up email to review what was discussed and ask if there are remaining questions or concerns. In addition, if someone sounds different during a call, I will call them afterwards to make sure they are okay.

I do not want to miss opportunities to interact and address potential individual issues. We must focus on assessing how people are doing beyond an employee survey; keeping in close touch with our people is how we will achieve the business results we seek.

THE CHANGE MAKERS

Ricky Torain is Executive Director of Quality at DRiV Incorporated. In this role, he is charged with developing, standardizing, and aligning quality strategies to create and implement a "zero defects" culture in a manufacturing environment.

CHAPTER 3

KNOW YOUR AUDIENCE AND THEIR NEEDS

COMMUNICATION HAPPENS
IN THE MIND OF THE_____:

A)
SENIOR LEADER

B)
SENDER

C)
LISTENER

D)
A AND B

E)
ALL OF THE ABOVE

THE ANSWER IS:
LISTENER

The listener decides whether you have communicated or not. They are the ones who decide whether you have created mutual understanding, built trust, and motivated someone to act. A trap leaders often fall into is to communicate from their perspective. After all, we're very clear what we think in our heads!

What's more, employees today are bombarded with so much information that it's hard for them to digest it all. They're bombarded with information but starved for meaning.

To truly move employees to action, we have to know what they care about and get into their mindset. During times of crisis and change, this can be especially challenging, with emotions understandably running high, as we saw during the COVID-19 crisis. Uncertainty can sometimes lead to feelings of helplessness, hopelessness, fear, heightened anxiety, and more. Think back to how you were feeling as COVID-19 first hit. As we transitioned to shelter-in-place and businesses closed, as people lost jobs because of the uncertainty, got sick and passed away, we all tried to make sense of the unrest that swept the U.S., and the world.

The core principle as we think about moving people to action is this—the more you know about someone, the better you can listen to them, empathize, support, or guide them in the direction you need them to go.

KNOW YOUR AUDIENCE

WHO IS YOUR AUDIENCE?

Who are you trying to reach/influence?

INTERNAL:
- My direct reports
- Project teams
- My boss
- Other functions
- Managers/supervisors
- Senior leadership
- Board of Directors
- Vendors/suppliers

EXTERNAL:
- Media/industry analysts
- Wall Street/financial analysts
- Government/regulators
- Customers
- Community
- Others?

WHERE ARE THEY COMING FROM?

- What concerns or issues do they have that might pose a challenge or risk?
- What positive perceptions do they hold that can be leveraged to increase chances of success?

WHAT ARE THEIR INFORMATION NEEDS?

- What do they currently know/ understand about your topic?
- What don't they know that will be critical to getting them engaged?
- How do they like to receive information?
- What barriers exist that may prevent them from supporting the topic?

TO DOWNLOAD THIS FREE TOOL, SEE PAGE 339

WHAT DO YOU WANT THEM TO:

THINK

If your audience thinks positively about a topic, they are more likely to feel positive. THINK is about the rational, factual and objective.

FEEL

If your audience feels positively about a topic, they are more likely to take action to support the topic. FEEL is about the emotional, intuitive and subjective.

DO

If your audience takes action to support your topic, you've successfully engaged them. Without this engagement, there won't be any change in behavior to support you.

_____

_____

_____

_____

_____

_____

_____

_____

_____

_____

_____

_____

THE 8 KEY QUESTIONS

Employees' fundamental needs

Whether employees actually ask them or not, there are always several key questions on their minds, especially during times of crisis. We call them The 8 Key Questions All Employees Have.

These questions are inspired by the famous psychology theory behind human motivation, Maslow's Hierarchy of Needs. That theory states that people need to fulfill their basic level of needs first before moving to more complex levels of thought or skill. In other words, you can't build a house or write a novel if you're literally starving or haven't slept in weeks. This obviously is true for employees. If they're dealing with a lot of unsatisfied basic needs—the "me-focused" needs—those have to be addressed first before employees can begin to think beyond themselves.

8. How can I help? ⎤
7. What's our vision and values? ⎥
6. How are we doing? ⎥ **WE**
5. What's our business strategy? ⎦

4. What's going on? —————— **TRANSITION**

3. Does anyone care about me? ⎤
2. How am I doing? ⎥ **ME**
1. What's my job? ⎦

Moving from 'me' to 'we'

Once employees feel their questions have at least been addressed, if not completely taken care of, they become more aware of the changes or initiatives happening outside their department or function and can ask the bigger question, "What's going on?" This is a transitional question that helps take employees from "me" to "we."

From there, they can begin to feel part of the larger organizational team and work together to accomplish key goals, even in the midst of remaining uncertainty and change. The ultimate payoff is when employees ask, "How can I help?" This is an expression of engagement—a willingness to do more—which also demonstrates a strong emotional connection to the organization.

Research also shows that leaders who meet their employees' strategic communication needs don't need to be the most stellar presenters or best listeners. When their intangible needs are met, employees will cut leaders slack.

Working through change

It's important to remember that The 8 Key Questions are questions employees think about, and perhaps ask, *every day*—whether they are new to the organization or veterans. When change happens, employees immediately go back to the me-focused questions. For example, an employee will naturally go straight back to the me questions when critical things happen inside the company, such as layoffs or job restructurings.

These types of moments will naturally prompt questions:

- Your company just furloughed 400 employees, or there's a major change or a decline in production and there's concern that it will impact work hours and/or working conditions

- Your division is being restructured

- There's a leadership shakeup and your boss is leaving the company

- As a person of color, you're concerned about incidents that seem to demonstrate a lack of understanding of issues facing minority employees

The leader's role

In today's environment, events will naturally trigger employees to go back to the bottom of the pyramid far more often than in the past. Still, it's the leader's job to keep moving employees through the questions and get back to the top of the questions pyramid as quickly as possible. When leaders aren't successful doing that, employees can get caught in what we call the valley of despair. Understandably, in that valley work gets interrupted, slows or even stops. All of this means there's a need for much more regular and more personal communications, especially as there's new information coming in. So, who handles what levels of communication?

COMMS TEAM:

Generally, the communications team through all its vehicles—the intranet, town halls, all-employee messages and more—can answer the key corporate questions on behalf of the organization, the we-focused questions.

LEADERS:

Leaders play a major role in answering the me-focused questions. Leaders need to know that this kind of communication is too important to be simply handed over to the communications department. Leaders must help answer the critical questions employees have about their job and how they contribute.

EMPLOYEES:

Since communication is a two-way street, employees also play as critical a role as leaders. Consider effective communication like a contact sport—everyone needs to participate. When employees have a question, they need to ask it. If employees don't know certain information to do their jobs, they need to seek it out.

06

LISTEN CLOSELY TO THE FRONT-LINE VOICE

I am currently the Program Director of the International Aerospace Environmental Group, a non-profit organization of global aerospace companies that collaborates on innovative solutions for environmental challenges facing our industry. Much of my career experience prior to this role has been leading organizations in Quality, Manufacturing, Supply Chain and Environment, Health and Safety. In addition to the U.S., I've worked, lived in and led teams in Sweden, The Netherlands, U.K., Malaysia and Japan.

Through my experiences, I've learned an important leadership lesson—never underestimate the power of the people closest to the work to come up with the solutions. This means spending a lot of time out of the office and talking with

people on the shop floor, seeking their input on what's working and what's not. It also means a lot of regular, consistent communication—often daily stand-up meetings with the entire team in the morning, followed by a second meeting in the afternoon to recap progress made and ongoing needs.

It's also very important to understand that different people react differently to ideas for change. Some have done well and even been promoted within an existing system and processes and are skeptical that change is even needed. Before any leader can get a team to embrace a proposed change, they first need to understand the different perspectives of the team—through very close listening.

An experience I had leading a team in Malaysia drives this point home.

There had been an injury to one of our employee's hands. As a result, about a third of the team refused to work and left the factory. I spoke to one of the group's natural leaders and asked about the situation. As it turned out, the whole group was convinced that the factory was cursed by an evil spirit. My belief system was different from theirs, but I knew that didn't matter. I asked what we could do and it was suggested that we invite a Feng Shui monk to visit.

I spent the day with the monk and noted his recommendations, which included making some minor changes to pillars at the front entrance, and also burying some small prayer rollers on the compound. For two of them, we had to dig a hole through a meter of reinforced concrete floor. While this required some effort, it paid off. There were no more concerns from the workforce after this was complete. Rather, I felt the team became even closer.

Through the experience, I learned a lot about the local culture and was inspired to take a course in Feng Shui. I felt the basic concept of "flow of energy" made a lot of sense when laying out floor plans for an office or home. As this experience shows, the front-line voice carries a lot more wisdom and power than I ever could have imagined at the time. And it has inspired me every time I'm about to consider a critical change within any group I lead today.

THE CHANGE MAKERS

Christer Hellstrand is Program Director of the International Aerospace Environmental Group and helps shape environmental policies impacting the aerospace industry. He previously served as Director of Environment, Health and Safety for Boeing Commercial Airplanes.

MEETING CHALLENGES FROM A PLACE OF TRUST, EMPLOYING AN INDIVIDUALIZED APPROACH

Trust between leaders, managers and employees is the cornerstone of successful communications. When change happens, large or small, a foundation of trust is what will move an organization more efficiently and effectively through the situation. Intentional and strategic attention by leaders to create, build and maintain this trust takes time, energy and commitment; it's worth every bit of effort. It's trust that inspires employees to work with leaders to identify and understand the challenges that may be faced. Then, and perhaps most importantly, trust helps teams find ways to move to action together and address challenges head on with creativity and courage. Innovation and new solutions come forth when trust guides the work. Trust is not easily won, and an individualized approach can be a good way to build a trusting partnership.

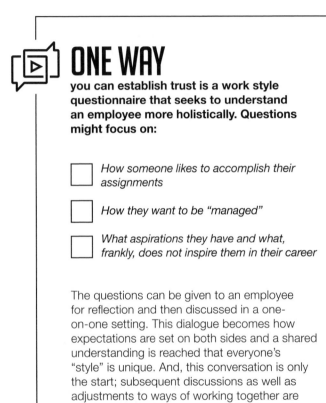

ONE WAY

you can establish trust is a work style questionnaire that seeks to understand an employee more holistically. Questions might focus on:

☐ *How someone likes to accomplish their assignments*

☐ *How they want to be "managed"*

☐ *What aspirations they have and what, frankly, does not inspire them in their career*

The questions can be given to an employee for reflection and then discussed in a one-on-one setting. This dialogue becomes how expectations are set on both sides and a shared understanding is reached that everyone's "style" is unique. And, this conversation is only the start; subsequent discussions as well as adjustments to ways of working together are all steps on the journey to more fulfilling and meaningful workplaces for everyone.

Erin Loverher is Senior Manager, Corporate Communications for Walgreens. In her role, she focuses on building a solid and consistent brand reputation both internally and externally. She directs strategic media relations initiatives that support corporate directions and counsels leaders on the alignment of key messaging.

7 THINGS
EVERY EMPLOYEE WANTS
FROM THEIR BOSS

Beyond needs, employees also have wants. Look at these wants as a complement to The Eight Key Questions employees have. What do employees want? While the answer varies by employee, our research and work reveals a collective "wish list" every boss should know. What follows are some of the most sought-after employee wants and those that come up most often as unmet...

TAKE ACTION 1 ON EMPLOYEE SUGGESTIONS

The action might be to loop back with the employee to share appreciation for their thoughts, and help them understand why you are or are not implementing their suggestion. By doing so, you're closing the feedback loop, which can be as worthwhile as implementing an employee's suggestion. Either way, you're saying that what they shared was valuable. This will motivate them

RECOGNIZE 2 AND SHOW APPRECIATION

Say "thank you" for a job well done. Reinforce very specifically the behaviors you want to continue to see. At a two-way communication training recently, a woman asked whether she needed to reward and recognize someone on her team for "just doing their job." Absolutely. Jobs don't inspire and motivate people; leaders do

3 LESS BS AND MORE HUMANITY

Enough beating-around-the-bush, or worse yet, "spinning" of messages. Employees want to know what's happening and why in a direct way. Tell them what you know when you know it. Chances are, you're currently waiting too long after getting key information to communicate.

4 EMPATHIZE WITH THEM

Pause and imagine how they're feeling. Show you hear them and validate their feelings. The payoff is an employee who knows you care; at the same time, you gather information that's useful to motivate that employee.

5 MORE LISTENING (TO THEM)

Stop talking so much. Ask for input and feedback. Employees are more likely to support things they help create. Stop the monologues and talking at them; have real, two-way conversations.

6
UNDER-STANDING YOUR EXPECTATIONS

People rise to the expectations set for them. Many problems in business are caused by a lack of understanding of expectations or a misunderstanding of what's needed and expected. Have you developed and articulated your expectations?

7
SHOW EMPLOYEES YOU CARE (IN A GENUINE WAY)

There's a myriad of ways to do this. Find out what's on their mind, what's essential and remember critical milestones that are important to employees.

08

FOSTER A GENUINE "EMPLOYEE FIRST" CULTURE

Many organizations today claim to be committed to an "employee-first culture," but I believe more work needs to be done before many can make that claim. Naturally, it takes much more than words. Whenever I take on a new leadership role, I try to ask insightful questions that will help provide a clear picture of the current organizational culture. To get to the heart of what is truly being done across every level of the organization, my questions traditionally center around the "why" behind current employee programs, engagement platforms and initiatives. What's the true purpose of this program? How are we engaging our people? How is leadership owning this and setting the tone? What's the impact?

Raising these questions and having this important, transparent dialogue has been extremely valuable for me

as a new leader, but what I take from this experience is the importance of continuing to ask questions even as you grow familiar and comfortable with an organization. Don't lose that 2-year-old inside you who never stops asking why. Asking the hard questions, listening, gathering feedback from all corners of the organization, and reflecting on the responses is what helps build a genuine employee-first approach and, empathetic communication platform.

The corporate "voice" then becomes more reflective of an employee-first mindset because it's actually influenced by your employees. Along with the tone, the frequency and consistency— the regular cadence—of your internal communication efforts is an essential component of employees feeling heard and cared about. In my new role as Chief Communication Officer for ABM

Industries, I'm also focused on the power of compelling storytelling, and leveraging this approach to cultivate the role of brand ambassadors at every communication touchpoint. Storytelling is a powerful communication tool, especially in times of change when employees are searching for context, meaning and a clear sense of purpose to their work.

Finally, it's important for leaders to ask the tough and uncomfortable questions in times of crisis as well. Following the recent senseless acts of racial injustice, I shared during a bias training session at my previous employer my personal experience as a minority and a Latin woman in leadership. I then challenged every leader in the session to set aside time to truly listen and spend time with their colleagues of color on the topic of racial inequality. I emphasized how important this was, sharing that none of us can really understand what is on people's minds until we ask. During that training, I also shared this:

> **TAKE ME. I'M A PERSON OF COLOR, MY HUSBAND IS CHINESE, MY BROTHER-IN-LAW IS AFRICAN AMERICAN, MY NEPHEW IS BROWN, AND MY AUNT IS JEWISH. DESPITE MY BACKGROUND, I HAVE NO IDEA WHAT IT IS LIKE TO BE AN AFRICAN AMERICAN IN THIS COUNTRY RIGHT NOW, AND I AM THE MOST DIVERSE PERSON HERE.**

The comment caused some of my colleagues to think harder about listening to different perspectives and I know many took action to do so. These hard conversations are critical to move forward and drive impactful change.

Nadeen Ayala is currently Chief Communication Officer for ABM Industries. In a distinguished career as a senior communications leader, she has previously served as Senior Vice President of Communication & Branding for Wiley, and as Senior Vice President of Global Communications for Wyndham Hotels & Resorts, among other roles.

09

BRING PEOPLE WITH YOU

In a previous position I held before coming to ServiceMaster Brands, I took on a new role that felt like a stretch at the time. The team I was given the opportunity to lead was embarking on a transformation. We needed to change how we delivered value to the organization as well as change how other teams perceived us. The key word here is change. Even though change is inevitable, it doesn't make it any easier to accept. And there are typically two paths to driving change as a leader — one is the politically savvy, emotionally intelligent approach, and the other is the "bull in a china shop" approach.

To help prepare myself for this journey, I read a few books about transformational leadership and reflected a lot on previous transformations I had witnessed from the outside looking in.

One thing seemed to be true for the ones that were successful — they brought people along the journey with them. That might sound simple, but it actually takes a lot of practice. It also requires letting go of the belief that you, as the leader, have to have all the answers.

As I began in that role, I heard a lot about what needed to change from other leaders, but I still wanted to form my own opinion. I asked what others valued most about the team today and what they felt we could do better — just as I would approach a close friend or family member if we realized something needed to change. I wanted to give my co-workers that same respect. After all, we are all humans with a desire to connect on a more genuine level.

"WE ARE ALL HUMANS WITH A DESIRE TO CONNECT ON A MORE GENUINE LEVEL.

What I found by approaching the change this way is that I built a coalition of supporters and a network I could trust to share feedback honestly along the way. Not only did this make driving change much easier but it helped create a community. While we still had work to do in that transformation journey, we created a step change that set a new level of expectation for the team.

This kind of open, humble and vulnerable approach to driving change helped set that team on the path to transformation. It also helped transform the team's relationships with other teams. By using the common ground we all shared, we all learned and grew stronger together. That experience has shaped the way I view leadership in profound ways and carries over to how I'm approaching my new role with ServiceMaster Brands.

Megan Booker is Senior Director of Communications at ServiceMaster Brands. She previously served in communications leadership roles at Anheuser-Busch InBev and Kimberly-Clark.

140

WHAT EMPLOYEES WANT
(AND NEED) TODAY

There's a common theme among many of the conversations I've been having with senior leaders about what employees want today in our world of working virtually—and that's more social connection. I'm not talking about more posts and tweets and texts, oh my! The desire is for real connectedness with another human being, which studies have shown can increase health and well-being.

*I **SEE** YOU. AND YOU **SEE** ME!*

Today, it's critical for leaders to respond to employees in new ways. As we continue to re-tool the way we work and respond to ongoing challenges in business and in our world, here's some of the top things on the wish list:

- To hear a familiar voice

- To see a friendly face, even via video

- To talk about what's challenging us… and conversely, what's bringing us joy

- To give someone the gift of being present and just listening

- To give others our support and empathy

- To laugh or cry or vent

In the end, to be human. And to have the space and the ability to "be" as we are, and be seen by others, which can fill our buckets.

5 STEPS TO SHOW YOU CARE

Now more than ever, leaders play a pivotal role in connecting, calming and inspiring their teams. Even as you and your organization are challenged during this time of uncertainty and change, employees also have a lot on their minds, and often a mix of emotions about themselves, their families and their work situation. A little empathy and thoughtful communication can go a long way to help employees know you care. Here are some simple, yet powerful, steps you can take to show employees they are cared for:

1 BE VISIBLE AND COMMUNICATE FREQUENTLY

Personal touchpoints are important to show people you understand their need to stay connected and informed. Engage with each team member at least once a week, whether in a daily huddle, a regular team meeting, 1:1 meeting or team conversations.

2 CHECK ON HOW THEY ARE DOING PERSONALLY

Talk with employees about what's happening in their daily lives outside of work, including personal interests, family news or how they are managing current circumstances. Especially if they are working remotely, employees have fewer opportunities to interact with each other casually, as they would at work, and this is a way to help them feel that personal connection.

3 DEMONSTRATE YOU CARE WITH LISTENING AND EMPATHY

In times of uncertainty, people need to feel heard and supported, and you can help by listening carefully to what employees have to say, imagining how they are feeling and expressing support. Reflect back what you hear and show sensitivity to their needs, offering help or guidance where you can.

4 TALK ABOUT WHAT MATTERS TO THEM, INCLUDING THE LITTLE THINGS

Whether employees ask them or not, there are always questions on their minds about how they are doing, what's expected of them, and what's happening in the organization. Keeping these top of mind as you provide direction and input to their work lets them know you are considering their needs. But it doesn't have to be all about work. Ask about plans or family events they've talked about or a TV show you both like. Showing you care includes talking about the fun stuff, too.

5 SHOW APPRECIATION FOR THEM AND WHAT THEY DO

Be sure to say thank you when they've been responsive or helpful, and share specific appreciative feedback on their work. And remember their birthdays, work anniversaries and other important dates—consider putting these dates in your calendar as a reminder to help your team members feel cared about and appreciated.

When employees are engaged and inspired, they drive productivity, business growth and the success of your organization as a whole. And you can sleep a little better knowing you're doing all you can to help employees weather the storm.

TIP: HERE'S WHAT EMPLOYEES SAY MANY MANAGERS _DON'T_ DO. {AND WISH THEY WOULD}

They Don't:

- Keep employees informed

- Explain the "why" behind decisions

- Communicate frequently enough and in a timely way

- Update employees on changes happening in the business

- Share regular business updates and how the team is performing

- Ask for feedback

- Ask for or listen to concerns

- Act on feedback (or at least close the loop as to why feedback wasn't incorporated into a decision)

- Demonstrate to employees that they care about them (or don't demonstrate empathy for their employees' situations)

CHANGE

THE WAY YOU TALK ABOUT THINGS, AND THE THINGS YOU TALK ABOUT WILL CHANGE

You often can resolve a negative situation by changing the context and your delivery. Your words and actions set the tone for those who follow you and your lead:

Paint the picture of what's possible, help people imagine and live the success you're aiming for.

Think about the way you have been talking about a major initiative or project. Is it positive? Hopeful? Filled with energy? Cautious? Fearful? Doubtful? Rethink your delivery to inspire and uplift your team and be sure to celebrate early wins.

As you paint the picture of what's possible, it's important to be real and speak with candor. You may need to include a nod to the fact that the road ahead won't necessarily be easy. However, you can share with your team that by following the steps you've set together to achieve the vision, the team can definitely get there—and it will all be worth it.

If your approach to discussing business results leaves people feeling less than enthused, it's possible that you didn't paint the path forward as a team effort. If you change your approach to a team-inspiring one, you can watch the results change.

EVEN IN THE TOUGHEST OF TIMES, PAINT A PICTURE OF WHAT'S POSSIBLE

In times of change, it's natural for people to feel so overwhelmed emotionally that they're paralyzed with inaction, feeling unsure about the best next step to take. But I think in turbulent times, it's especially important to remind people of the collective agency we have to manage through a crisis together. It's about reinforcing the idea that we're not all just helpless bystanders, but, in fact, there are actions that we can take. For instance, in times of racial unrest, it's possible to work toward building a more inclusive culture inside the company—modeling what you'd like to see more broadly in the world.

Sometimes putting situations into context also helps. The crisis we've gone through over the past year has clearly been multifaceted. There's not just been the pandemic but tremendous social and political upheaval as well. But we've faced similar moments of crisis in our history. When you think about times of crisis in the past—such as World War 1 and the ensuing 1918 pandemic—those critical moments also led to incredible innovation and progress over time, such as advances in public health and technology that were game-changing for generations.

So as tragic as some of these events are for us right now, I'm also trying to look for the opportunities that may be ahead of us; the ways that we may find ourselves changing for the better out of the necessity of the moment. I believe as leaders that's a useful and important way to help our teams navigate a very difficult time.

> **AS PART OF THIS, THE WORD CURIOSITY COMES TO MIND. THE IDEA THAT RATHER THAN LETTING THE CONFUSION TAKE HOLD OF YOU, LET THE CONFUSION BREED CURIOSITY BECAUSE THAT'S WHERE THE INVENTIONS, THE INNOVATIVE SOLUTIONS—AND THE HOPE—ULTIMATELY LIES.**

Paula Angelo
is Vice President, Internal & CEO Communications at The Hartford. Paula and her team provide internal communication counsel and coaching for the company's senior team, including the CEO. She also provides thought leadership on the use of digital channels for internal communications and how best to foster engagement and innovation among team members.

HOW TO CHECK IN

with your people about social unrest and other difficult topics

Talking about systemic racism is one of the most difficult conversations to have, and each new unfortunate incident of racism brings its own set of challenges and emotions. To not have a conversation or acknowledge an incident of social unrest, or another hugely difficult topic, sends a message in itself.

Employees will interpret your silence as meaning that you don't care, don't find the topic important, or don't know how to talk about it. While a protest centered on racial unrest or frustrations about the lack of diversity in an organization might be difficult to discuss, the goal isn't to have a perfect conversation or to solve the issue. Rather, you want to be there for your team as they try and make sense of what's going on. With any difficult topic, you want them to feel that their voice is important and ideally send a message that you care, and when appropriate, we're all in this together.

A human connection is needed, and that involves purely listening

A core question that most effective leaders ask of themselves and others is this: How can I help? Today, we can listen and help our employees express and process their emotions, whatever they are, as a means of caring and showing your support for them during challenging moments inside the business—or for the country. One-on-one check-ins are one of the most effective ways to understand where others are coming from, and to show you care.

THE CONVERSATION-STARTER MIGHT SOUND SOMETHING LIKE THIS:

Given what's happening now, I'm checking in with everyone on the team individually, as I've done when we've faced tough times before. If it's helpful to you, I'm open to listening to how you're feeling to help you process all that's going on. If you'd prefer not to talk about it, that's okay, too. Just know I'm always here to listen to you. 🗮

You know best who to start with as you prioritize these conversations. Think about who might be most impacted, or who might have the strongest feelings, and where you can help. The goal is to listen and help your employees feel heard. Chances are, you will hear various interpretations of facts and emotions—some of which you might agree with, and others that you might strongly disagree with.

A time of global, national or organizational crisis is an important moment to express your point-of-view. This is not about you; rather, this is about helping your employees feel heard so you can understand where others are coming from, and can genuinely help, if there's something you can do.

HOW DO I FIT IN?

In addition to The Eight Key Questions (see page 125), another way to engage employees in the larger goals of the company, especially during times of change and challenge, is to help employees personalize strategy and understand how they fit in. This is really about helping them feel appreciated and valued.

I often share the story of two brick layers who were hard at work. When asked what they were doing, the first brick layer said:

I'M BUILDING A WALL

When the other was asked, he said:

I'M BUILDING A CASTLE

BOTH ARE DOING THE SAME TASK;
YET, THEIR MINDSET AND THEREFORE,
HOW THEY FEEL IS DIFFERENT.

Employees need to know both their wall, and their castle:

 What they do (this is the wall): "I work in a manufacturing plant and I help us make (masks, component parts for the vaccine, chips, etc.)."

 How they contribute (this is their castle): "What I'm really doing right now is helping to save lives during the pandemic."

Big picture, we need more employees helping us build the castle, not just the wall. The benefits are many—to ensure that employees best efforts are helping achieve the organization's strategy, as well as to help them know that the work they're doing matters. This is especially important during a crisis. Employees want to know they're making a contribution to the larger whole, which helps drive engagement.

HELP EMPLOYEES ARTICULATE HOW THEY FIT IN

The goal is that employees can articulate how they fit in. Note that this isn't about thinking they already know, but being able to talk about the contributions they make. Sometimes the dialogue—and the thought process that goes with it—can lead to improved focus on what matters most and improved performance. To get there, employees need to understand how they contribute to the organization's success. First, they need a fundamental understanding of what's important to the organization, including:

| THE ORGANIZATION'S VISION AND MISSION | ITS STRATEGY, IN THE CONTEXT OF THE BUSINESS ENVIRONMENT TODAY | THE OVERALL GOALS OF THE ORGANIZATION | MOST IMPORTANT, THE OVERALL GOALS OF THEIR TEAM |

Try this exercise at your next staff meeting

How do you think your employees would do at answering these questions?
Try this exercise: Tell your employees that you want to ensure everyone is
understanding the valuable role that they play in contributing to your organization's
success. After all, your team rocks! Here are 6 steps to success:

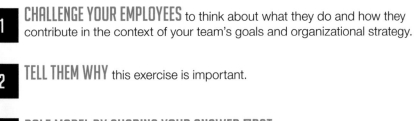

1 CHALLENGE YOUR EMPLOYEES to think about what they do and how they
contribute in the context of your team's goals and organizational strategy.

2 TELL THEM WHY this exercise is important.

3 ROLE MODEL BY SHARING YOUR ANSWER FIRST. Lead with your brilliance
and inspiration!

4 ASK YOUR EMPLOYEES TO WRITE DOWN THEIR ANSWERS. Tell them there
are no right or wrong answers.

5 HAVE EVERYONE SHARE one at a time what they came up with.
Promise thunderous applause!

6 ASK FOR FEEDBACK after everyone's turn on what works (celebrate!) and
what can be better about how a peer articulates how he or she fits in.

Chances are, many employees just see their tasks and not the bigger picture of
how they contribute. You also might learn that there's a need for your team to better
understand the organization's goals and strategy, too. Or, there's not clarity on
your team's priorities. No matter what the learnings, you've started an important
discussion that you can continue regularly, and can form the basis of lots of
celebration in the future. And what team can't use even more celebration?

CHAPTER 4

SHOW YOUR HUMAN SIDE

Understandably, leaders see people reacting very emotionally in uncertain or challenging times for an organization. In response, a little care and empathy can go a long way. That involves being present and listening, and finding other ways to show your human side.

Of course, there's an inherent challenge to showing the human side if you're not able to meet people face-to-face. In those situations, you may be relying too much on email. If you're not meeting employees as much as you'd like or know you should be during a time of change, it's important to work extra hard to make meaningful connections that allow you to support and maintain meaningful relationships. Think about the best ways to genuinely connect in other ways—hearing colleagues, having direct and transparent dialogue about what's important, and just doing a lot more listening than you might have in the past.

Empathy

A powerful way to show you care is to help others sort through their feelings and understand them, to show empathy. Empathy is ultimately about putting yourself in someone else's shoes and reflecting genuinely on what they are feeling. It's not about agreement; in fact, you don't have to agree with someone to empathize with them. You just need to play back what you're hearing so they feel heard.

The benefits of empathy are threefold:

- It helps others understand their own feelings—even the difficult ones—and enables them to reduce the chance of those feelings controlling them.

- Leaders who address the emotional content first help employees move to the more rational and more logical part of their brains.

- Logic leads to greater calmness for everyone and more confidence that leadership is the steady hand at the wheel. For today's anxious employees, that's a huge leadership win.

Here are some thoughtstarter suggestions to have a helpful and productive conversation. You can decide how to make these proven strategies "real" and authentic to how you lead:

1 LISTEN WITHOUT INTERRUPTION

Listen especially for and reflect the emotional content. Think: What are the feelings I'm hearing behind the words? Accept and validate the feelings you hear: "Sounds like this is very frustrating for you…"

2 PARAPHRASE WHAT YOU'RE HEARING TO DEMONSTRATE YOU'RE LISTENING

"What I hear you saying is…" "Let's me make sure I got this…" Again, you don't have to agree with the thinking; you just need to play back what you're hearing so the person feels heard.

3 HELP EMPLOYEES REALIZE THEY ARE NOT ALONE IF THEY'RE STRUGGLING

Talk about how everyone is sorting out a specific challenge at the same time. For example: "This situation is really difficult, hard and complex for all of us. We're all struggling with how we feel about it."

4 WRAP UP WHEN YOU SENSE THE EMPLOYEE IS FEELING HEARD

"I hope this will be an ongoing conversation." Share your appreciation for how they've opened up to you, and for the trust they've placed in you. Let the employee know the conversation is private and you're always available to continue the dialogue, if that's helpful.

Know that employees don't expect you to be perfect in how you handle this, or to have all the answers; just listen, be human, and real. Don't avoid the topic because it is hard and uncomfortable. Lead with heart and try to open up dialogue that's respectful, compassionate and helpful.

Q&A:

Thoughts on embracing an empathy mindset

Q:

As a leader, how do I show respect for people's challenges with any changes going on in the organization while still ensuring that projects and workstreams move forward?

A: It's an important question, and it's not an "either/or." I suggest we think about it as a "both/and" scenario. As leaders, we need to think about how we can be empathetic and understanding, and focus on what we need to do to move the business forward. I recommend doing check-ins with your folks to get a sense of their mindset and how they're feeling so you can meet them where they are. This is especially true during times of change and challenge. Helping people work through their feelings, and doing what you can to remove obstacles that are in their way, is going to be the most productive way to get them focused on the job at hand.

Q:

How do I respond to individuals on a team—including leaders—who lack empathy and don't make accommodations for employees facing special challenges during a time of crisis or change?

A:

It depends, in part, on your relationship with the individual who's demonstrating a lack of empathy. If this is a member of your team, you can reinforce the importance of empathy as a key tenet of leadership, and you can coach them on how to do it. You might ask about the person's ability to demonstrate empathy as you collect feedback on him or her from others and reflect that feedback in a performance review. This allows you to continue to help the person develop their aptitude for empathy. If the lack of empathy is coming from a peer or someone more senior to you, it can be more challenging. If possible, set up a one-on-one conversation with the peer and preface your comments with a statement such as, "I want to share some feedback I think is important but may be tough to hear. If it were me, I'd want to hear it." Share examples of times when the peer could have shown more empathy and how that could have benefited them. In the end, you can't control how someone reacts to your thoughtful feedback.

LEADERS:
Listen more now than ever before

You know who you are. You think listening is a soft skill and highly overrated. Or, you're confident that you're a good listener so you don't need to work on the skill and raise the bar. Or, you're a leader who thinks as the boss, your job is to "tell," as opposed to listen. Part of what's changed since the COVID-19 outbreak and recent experiences with social unrest is that the urgent need for leaders to listen to their employees and understand their challenges is very clear. Listening is one of the most important things you can do. It's a clear sign of respect for the person you're communicating with. The better we listen, the better we can understand one another.

When listening is done well and genuinely, it helps you get what you want.

The better you listen to others, the better they will listen to you. The better you listen, the more information and insights you can gather to guide how you work with colleagues, or lead productive and purposeful conversations with your team. The better you listen, the more you learn about your employees' needs, concerns and worries, which allows you to empathize and support them. When employees feel their needs are heard, acknowledged and addressed, they're more likely to feel part of an inclusive team that welcomes their unique experiences and provides a safe place to share their perspectives openly.

4 MOST COMMON BARRIERS

to effective listening

1. Thinking more about what you're saying than what you're hearing.

2. Deciding what you're going to say next before the person you're talking with finishes what they're saying.

3. Putting a higher priority on what you're saying than the person you're talking with.

4. Not working at listening. Working on your listening skills will help you meet your team's needs. Who is struggling? Who might need some time off to process everything that is going on?

11

PUT PEOPLE FIRST

Four thousand of our wholesalers, employees, Board members and reporters were making their way back to their seats in a packed Houston convention center as we wrapped up the second day of our annual distributor convention—the biggest single moment for our business each year. It's the gathering where new brands are launched, where ad campaigns are revealed, where the excitement generated hopefully translates into greater enthusiasm and greater sales.

As the leadership of Molson Coors Beverage Company, we couldn't have been happier. It had been less than four months since we launched a plan to revitalize our business, restructure our global organization and free up more money to invest in our brands. And it had been less than one month since we unveiled a new set of company values, starting with the core foundation: Put People First. Yet in that short time we were already starting to turn some doubters into believers—largely on the strength of exciting new investments beyond the beer aisle, new above premium priced products that would be growth drivers and the relative strength of our iconic core brands. February 26, 2020 was to be a milestone moment for

Molson Coors, and a critical point in our work to build confidence in the company and momentum for our brands—the primary goal for the communications and corporate affairs team. The convention was going incredibly well. The hall was filled with excitement and enthusiasm. One reporter in attendance called it, "one of the best Molson Coors distributor conventions in years." And we were about to close it out strong.

I was pacing the halls outside the staff room when someone grabbed me to let me know our General Counsel was looking for me. "Lee needs you." And I was ushered into an empty windowless conference room, with our CEO, our General Counsel and our head of security.

"There's an active shooter in our Milwaukee brewery."

Time stood still for a moment. Details were coming in fast minute-by-minute, though it never seemed fast enough. 4,000 people were mingling in the convention hall just below us. Most of them completely unaware of what was transpiring in one of our oldest and most historical breweries. We were now running late for the opening of the final session of the convention.

People were starting to wonder what was going on. What was the delay? There was no time to gather data. No time to make alternate plans. No time to wait. A small group of senior leaders were now gathered, and we made the call. The remainder of the convention was canceled. When our CEO stepped before the crowd in Houston, he briefly told them what we knew at the time. He apologized for cutting the convention short but made it clear that he needed to depart for Milwaukee immediately. Because the most important thing at that moment was not the new brands or campaigns.

The most important thing was to be with our people.

In that moment, with so much on the line, we were guided by that new company value: Put People First. And it remained at the center of every decision we made in the days and weeks that followed. When we arrived in Milwaukee later that evening and our CEO found out there were still a couple of employees who had to work inside the brewery that night for safety purposes, very quietly he personally went to offer his condolences and

thank them for being there in such a difficult time. When employees gradually came back together at the brewery a few days later, leaders were there to offer their support and participate in small and large group discussions.

When media stories raised disturbing questions about other events inside our brewery, we openly acknowledged some historic challenges and committed to making meaningful improvements in the short and long term. And that is just what we have done in the time since.

Our work didn't end when the sun set on February 26, 2020. It didn't end a few weeks later when the glare of the TV cameras was no longer on us. In many ways it will never end. Because at the end of the day, we can only succeed — personally and professionally — when we put people first. It was a philosophy that guided us through an incredibly difficult time in our company's history. And it was a philosophy that we would quickly put to work again in the coronavirus pandemic, an incredibly difficult time in world history.

THE
CHANGE
MAKERS

Adam Collins is Chief Communications and Corporate Affairs Officer, Molson Coors Beverage Company.

WHAT LEADERS MISS
when they don't listen *(and what to do about it)*

Leaders, in particular, often forget to listen and fall into the trap of trying to control the message without seeking real, meaningful communication.

What we're missing when we don't listen:

- The opportunity to learn something new

- Insights that may help us be more effective

- Context, which helps us make sense of situations

- An alternative perspective

- The opportunity to demonstrate respect for another person (whether you agree with that person or not)

A few strategies for becoming a more effective communicator through better listening:

- Stop talking

- Suppress the inclination to think about what you are going to say next

- Don't multitask; focus closely on the speaker

- Ask questions to ensure you understand

- Paraphrase what you're hearing

- Listen with an open mind, not for what you want to hear

- Pay attention to what's not said

The reality is that the best communicators—and leaders—spend much of their time observing, absorbing and really listening to—*and hearing*—their employees.

SILENCE IS MORE THAN IT SEEMS

One of the greatest skills that any leader can master is becoming comfortable with silence. Many people view silence as empty space that needs to be filled, but when leaders learn to accept it—and work with it—they open the doors for others to speak and be heard. The result is often an unexpected and enlightening connection and a wealth of information.

1. APPROACH EACH DIALOGUE WITH THE GOAL TO LEARN SOMETHING.

Think of the person as someone who can teach you.

2. STOP TALKING AND FOCUS CLOSELY ON THE SPEAKER.

Suppress the urge to think about what you're going to say next or to multitask.

3. OPEN AND GUIDE THE CONVERSATION.

Open and guide the conversation with broad, open-ended questions such as: What other strategic alternatives did you consider? How do you envision...? Avoid closed-ended questions that can be answered with just a "yes" or "no."

4. DRILL DOWN TO THE DETAILS.

Drill down to the details by asking directive, specific questions that focus the conversation, such as: Tell me more about... How did you come to this conclusion? How would this work?

5. SUMMARIZE WHAT YOU HEAR AND ASK QUESTIONS TO CHECK YOUR UNDERSTANDING.

You can accomplish this with statements such as: If I'm understanding you... or Tell me if this is what you're saying....

6. ENCOURAGE WITH POSITIVE FEEDBACK.

If you can see that a speaker has some trouble expressing a point or lacks confidence, encourage him or her with a smile, a nod or a positive question to show your interest.

7. LISTEN FOR TOTAL MEANING.

Understand that in addition to what is being said, the real message may be non-verbal or emotional. Checking body language is one way to seek true understanding.

8. PAY ATTENTION TO YOUR RESPONSES.

Remember that the way you respond to a question also is part of the dialogue. Keep an open mind and show respect for the other person's point of view even if you disagree with it.

12

GLAD TO BE HERE

Leading through change is always a challenge, but what I've discovered is that attitude goes a long way toward helping your team accomplish any goal, no matter the size or scope. Working through the pandemic has to be the toughest challenge we've faced from a change management perspective within our company—it's change management on steroids. In moments like these, I find myself reflecting back on this famous Theodore Roosevelt quote: "People don't care how much you know, until they know how much you care." Everything I've done in my career as a manager or leader stems from that premise; it's my single largest leadership philosophy.

I try to carry this message forward for my team, and even for my three college-aged children: Whoever you work with, whatever your role, you have someone you serve—everyone has a customer, whether that's external to your organization or inside of it, you serve someone. And you really need to get good at demonstrating that you care with those people. Unfortunately, many people don't run their lives like that. They oftentimes dismiss the emotional intelligence piece. But I genuinely believe that caring is the key to growing your business or advancing any project.

In leading my team, I try to demonstrate that it's all the little things you do that show you care. For instance, I'm a big "name"

guy. I make a concerted effort to remember people's names. So many people find it acceptable to just say, "Forgive me, I'm bad with names." Yet remembering someone's name is a demonstration that you care about them, and you value your connection to them. I tell my kids this too—remember everyone's name, the clerk at the grocery store who you see every week, the barista at the coffee shop, the classmate you see in the lecture hall week after week. It all matters. I just think it's an important lens into someone's character. If someone spends the time to get to know my name, that's the first step to showing me that they care.

Good leadership also requires me to take stock of where my team is on a personal level. During the pandemic, it was paramount to know about my team's family lives to understand what support they might need from me. For instance, parents of young children with no child care options during quarantine needed us to rethink the times for our meetings. In fact, we did an entire audit of all the regular calls in our schedules and pruned the times wherever we could to accommodate dynamic calendars. Some calls were cut down to 15 minutes, and others were moved away from busy family times. Doing this freed up critical space in the day for folks to get their work done efficiently while balancing their personal obligations. The pandemic forced this, but candidly this should have been done anyway. Getting people in a really good place mentally gives the team so much more firepower because people feel they're in a work environment where people care and they'll do their best work.

I learned some of this "show that you care" from my first leadership role many years ago, when I was in an entry level manager job. It quickly became clear to me that culture was everything. If people felt like work was a chore, they just weren't going to give anything extra or invest fully in the work. So many businesses struggle with this concept, yet it's so important: Create a culture which ensures that when colleagues walk in the door or hop on a video call, they're feeling valued, understand our purpose, feel safe, and can operate in a really good place.

During times of change—such as the pandemic and the racial unrest that followed—I tried to keep an even closer ear out for people's needs, and sense when they needed a break. There were moments when it was clear that the team was working really hard and "redlining" (a term we use describing when a car begins to shake because it is continually in overdrive). As leaders we have to give people permission to unplug, and feel safe in doing so. We

recently had a virtual meeting after a particularly stressful week where it was no agenda, bring your adult beverage, have your kid or pet make a cameo on the video, talk and support one another, and simply be together as a team in a very light and supportive setting. It filled the spirit banks.

Some of my inspiration for this approach comes from a corporate leadership expert named John Foley. He's a retired pilot with the U.S. Navy Blue Angels and has worked with corporate teams like ours to offer motivational guidance. At our sales team meeting with John, he showed up with a T-shirt with the words: "Glad to Be Here." It was about his philosophy—and mine too—that in any initial meeting with people, you need to be sure you give the clear impression that you're glad to be with them. It completely changes the outcome of the encounter when you take that approach.

It may seem like such a small thing, but it's not. Leaders need to think about the vibe they're sending in their actions and in their words. When you show that you care, when you're "glad to be here," you're that much closer to bringing your team along with you, regardless of the challenge.

THE CHANGE MAKERS

Tim Fagan
is SVP and Chief Revenue Officer at TEGNA, an innovative media company with 64 television stations in 51 markets, reaching nearly 40 percent of television households nationwide. Prior to joining TEGNA in 2013, Tim held leadership positions at various digital media businesses including HomeFinder.com, Apartments.com, and Classified Ventures.

13

LISTEN CLOSELY, AND WITH EMPATHY

In times of change, the most important thing I've learned is to make yourself available to listen with empathy and connect authentically. One of the ways my company accomplishes that goal is by running a quarterly employee survey, which we've increased in frequency during the pandemic to get a better sense for how employees are feeling. Given how fluid things are in the COVID world and how employees are mostly still working from home, the surveys give managers a good perspective on the current mood to allow them to quickly identify any common questions or concerns. We share the results with our team and discuss ways we can do better. This enables a constant feedback loop, which is a fantastic way to connect deeply with the team. I also feel it's important to recognize that your team may be dealing with uncertainty or doubt, and it's important to frequently ask the simple question: "How are you?" In doing so, it's helpful to share how you feel as well to help open up the conversation. By creating a safe environment for employees to share their concerns, leaders can help build a greater understanding of their team's

challenges and foster a dialogue that's empathetic and relevant to employees' needs. In times of rapid change, leaders also need to confront issues that aren't typical business-as-usual challenges and bring those concerns to senior management so the right actions can be taken for the benefit of the full team. While the importance of one-on-one check-ins are important, leaders should remember to share overall feedback with the broader team to drive a collective understanding of team level concerns. Leaders can then communicate a progress plan and create regular milestones to check in so that they're capturing shifts and new changes as the situation evolves.

THE MOST IMPORTANT THING

is for your team to feel that while changes are afoot, there is transparency and a forum to connect whether at a group or individual level. Most importantly, your team needs to know that they will be heard and treated with empathy.

Liru Chan
is Head of Marketing for Visa in Singapore. In this role, she is responsible for driving creative and impactful marketing strategies aimed at increasing brand vitality and positive results for Visa's business in Singapore. She has more than 15 years' experience in marketing and public relations and is highly skilled at building and managing high performing teams.

STRATEGIES
to be a better listener

A great tool for being a better listener is reflective listening, which lets the listener know you're listening and hearing them, and also encourages people to elaborate as they process their thoughts and feelings.

Actively hear and understand what others are saying without judgment. Approach each dialogue with the goal of learning something. Think: "I can learn something from this person."

Stop talking and focus closely on the speaker. Suppress the urge to multitask or focus on what you are going to say next. Be in this moment, not the next.

Reflect back the thoughts and feelings you're hearing in your own words. You don't want to parrot exactly what was said. Rather, repeat the message in your own words, paraphrase, or reflect feelings.

Remember that playing back what someone says doesn't necessarily mean you agree. Instead, it demonstrates that you hear them, and you understand what they're feeling.

EXAMPLES OF REFLECTIVE LISTENING

- After hearing concerns from an employee that a rotation schedule (one week at work, one week at home) is very taxing, play back their message and add: "I hear that the schedule is really challenging for you. And I can tell it's reinforcing your worry about the security of your job."

- Once you address the emotional content (acknowledge the challenge), you might then share what you know right now and don't know, which may offer some assurance, and also help the person feel a little more recognized and understood.

- In the end, the goal is to better understand where someone is coming from and help them sort through their feelings so they can focus on the meaningful work you need them to accomplish.

LISTENING QUIZ

TO DOWNLOAD THIS FREE TOOL, SEE PAGE 339

Ask one of your direct reports, your boss, or anyone with whom you communicate to honestly respond yes or no to these 10 questions:

	YES	NO
1. During the past few weeks, can you recall a time where you thought I wasn't listening to you?		
2. When you are talking to me, does my interaction with you make you feel stressed?		
3. When you talk to me, do I tend to lose eye contact with you?		
4. Do I ever get defensive when you tell me things I disagree with?		
5. When talking to me, does the conversation often end without me asking questions to clarify what you've said?		
6. In a conversation, do I sometimes overreact to information?		
7. Do I ever jump in to finish what you're saying?		
8. Is it common that I don't change my opinion after talking something over with you?		
9. When you are trying to communicate something to me, do I often talk too much?		
10. When you talk to me, do I ever seem distracted?		

Reflect on your "yes" answers and think about which one or two would have the greatest positive impact to help you listen even better?

3 ADVANCED LISTENING SKILLS

1 LISTENING FOR WHAT'S NOT SAID

When was the last time you were listening and picked up on something that was not said, such as a critical detail that was missing? *(See next page for more detail.)*

2 FLEXING YOUR STYLE

Do you adapt how you listen based on who you're speaking with? Introverts need more time to process, so with them, you may need to be more comfortable with some silence. By contrast, extroverts think out loud, so you need to spend more time paraphrasing back to ensure you understand the main point he or she is trying to make in a potentially long-winded and confusing way.

3 ASKING QUESTIONS THAT HELP GROUND YOU AT A STRATEGIC LEVEL

This is all about asking broad, probing, open-ended questions first, which allow you to take the conversation in a direction that gets at the main point.

You might ask:
- "Help me understand..."
- "How do you envision...?"
- "What's the outcome you seek?"
- "What other strategic alternatives did you consider?"

Next, ask more directive questions, which focus the conversation and get at additional specifics:
- "Tell me more about..."
- "How would this work?"
- "How did you come to this conclusion?"

As with any learned skill, you need to practice these strategies. Most people aren't born with the ability to ride a bike or to swim. Someone needs to show you how, and you then need to practice. As my high school music teacher said, "It's not practice that makes perfect. It's perfect practice that makes perfect." Glad I was listening when she said those words of wisdom.

STRATEGIES THAT WORK

to listen for what's *NOT* being said

How does one get better at paying attention to what's not being said? Let's look at a communication interaction from the sender and receiver's perspective.

A SENDER'S PERSPECTIVE

Here are some things that get in the way of a speaker sharing a clear message:

- They don't have the words or vocabulary, nor the emotional self awareness, to express what they're feeling and to get their needs out there

- Other times, they are afraid to express true thoughts or feelings

In both cases, when leaders don't know how to talk about a topic, the result is that they either avoid a topic, or communicate in vague terms that might seem irrelevant to a listener and get glossed over.

A LISTENER'S PERSPECTIVE

From a listener's perspective, what gets in the way?

- Leaders talk too much and don't listen enough

- Leaders listen to respond instead of listening to understand

- Leaders aren't listening for word clues or noticing body language that signify there's additional information that is yet to be uncovered

──── HOW TO ────
LISTEN BETTER FOR WHAT'S
NOT BEING SAID

- Be curious. If you're not a naturally curious person, think to yourself, "I'm curious about what this person has to say."

- Listen for the underlying issue or emotion (a fight about dirty clothes on the floor isn't about the clothes on the floor; there's a larger issue at play).

- Ask clarifying questions to ensure you understand before moving on from a topic. Listen and clarify. Repeat, as needed.

- Trust your gut if you're feeling like you're not getting the complete story.

- Notice any body language changes (i.e. change in position, facial movements), which may be a cue or clue to ask more questions.

- Listen for any emotional clues that signal there might be more to the story.

- When we communicate effectively, we understand where another person is coming from. If you don't understand where someone else is coming from (you don't need to agree with them), it means you need to ask more questions.

- Ask yourself in your own head during a pause in the conversation: "What's not being said?"

LISTEN AND CHECK
FOR UNDERSTANDING

ASK EMPLOYEES/SUPERVISORS, "WHAT AM I DOING WELL? HOW COULD I BE EVEN BETTER?"

Feedback:

_____

_____

_____

_____

_____

_____

_____

_____

Action plan to address:

_____

_____

_____

_____

_____

_____

TODAY: _____

NEXT 30 DAYS: _____

NEXT 90 DAYS: _____

TO DOWNLOAD THIS
FREE TOOL, SEE PAGE 339

6 STEPS TO BETTER CONNECT

1 HAVE REGULAR CHECK-INS ON THE CALENDAR

You and your employees decide what the frequency should be, and ensure they occur more often during times of change and challenge.

2 FIND OUT AND REMEMBER WHAT YOUR EMPLOYEES ARE PASSIONATE ABOUT

How would they spend a Saturday? At a museum? A concert? Do they golf?
Do they have a favorite sports team?

3 DEMONSTRATE YOU KNOW THE LITTLE THINGS THAT MATTER TO THEM

What might be on their minds as they come to work? Do they have a TV show they watch regularly, or one they've binge-watched recently?

4 REMEMBER THEIR BIRTHDAYS

Consider putting these dates in your calendar as a reminder.

5 INTERACT WITH THEM AS PEOPLE, AS COLLEAGUES

Employees are our colleagues, not our audience. Say hello. Ask them how their weekend went—and demonstrate active listening.

6 SAY THANK YOU AND SHARE SPECIFIC APPRECIATIVE FEEDBACK OFTEN

Focus on the behaviors you appreciate and want to see more of.

Q&A:

Is better listening actually doable for busy leaders?

Q:

You recommend checking in with everyone regularly. That would probably take up my whole day, every day if I did that.

How can I stay connected and satisfy the "me" items without connecting so often with everyone?

A:

If you have a large team, it's understandable that finding the time for check-ins is challenging. My recommendation is to set aside a certain amount of time (whether that is 30 minutes a day or an hour) and commit to spending it checking in on your people. During difficult times, it's likely that you'll figure out quickly who needs more of your time and attention because they are struggling with the "me" questions, like "How am I doing?" and "Does anyone care about me?" Others might be doing well and not require as frequent check-ins.

If you have direct reports who are supervising others on your team, you should set the expectation that they will check in with their team members and alert you if they need you to step in and help with someone who is having a hard time. Ultimately, my counsel is to do the best you can to stay in touch with your people and flex to meet their needs. Make it a priority because it is important for their ability to focus and be productive. And that's important to your success.

INSIGHTS

from inside companies: As a leader, embrace honesty and transparency

Many leaders see the power of being candid and open with their teams during difficult times of change or crisis, underscoring the fact that everyone is in this together. During the pandemic, some leaders spent time talking about what sheltering at home has been like for them and for their families, which helped break down barriers with their teams and encouraged more open discussions. Here are some of their thoughts:

I learned a long time ago that people can absorb and react appropriately to bad news if the content and the messenger are credible. Tell the truth. Be consistent. Rely on experts. Deal with facts. It's really not complicated. It starts with doing and saying what's right.

Be honest with people. Don't just repeat the company line. Share your personal concerns too and look for opportunities to be optimistic.

Being attentive to and acknowledging employees' feelings of fear and uncertainty about the pandemic and doing so genuinely will go a long way. You can even be vulnerable about your own apprehension and be calm and provide a reassuring voice.

CHAPTER 5

COMMUNICATE THE RIGHT MESSAGES AT THE RIGHT TIMES

I titled my first book "You Can't **NOT** Communicate," knowing the reality that leaders are communicating whether they intend to or not. How they spend their time, who they reward and recognize, what they talk about and focus on, who they associate with—it's all communication. We've all heard the phrase, "actions speak louder than words." It's absolutely true. People are watching our feet first and then listening to what we have to say. Plus, there's another variable at play—it's human nature for others to read into our actions based on their perceptions. So others attach meaning to our actions whether we like it or not, and the meaning they attach is based on them (not us!). It may or may not be in sync with what we intend.

So, my advice for leaders has always been this—if you're already communicating whether you want to or not, you might as well get better at it. And if others read into our actions, it benefits us to be even more planful and purposeful so we can be clear about our motivation and intent.

In uncertain times, everyone operates in minutes, hours and days, not weeks and months. That requires even more frequent communication. One of the most common barriers I hear from leaders is this sentiment: "I don't have time to communicate." It seems like this statement comes from a perception that there isn't enough time to draft a plan or that more work could be done and valuable time saved by not drafting a plan. Yet decades of experience tells us that this is not the case, and that was underscored by the experience of the pandemic.

One of the bright spots in the early days of the pandemic, and surrounding events of social unrest, was that we saw leaders and communication professionals step to the plate like never before. We saw the kind of focus and prioritization that most often only happens in a crisis. We regularly heard examples of how businesses changed virtually overnight to meet unprecedented global challenges. Program implementations that were slated for six months were completed in three weeks. Stalled priority projects were funded and introduced. As important, what wasn't absolutely critical was stopped dead in its tracks, as we've rarely seen before in business.

Leaders found the time to communicate smartly and strategically with their people in a myriad of ways. Check-ins. Small group discussions. Town halls. *Ask Me Anything* sessions. And more. And the business results have followed.

2 THINGS EFFECTIVE LEADERS DID:

1 Planned their communications

2 Ensured a smart communication cadence or rhythm to meet the needs of the team and business

TAKE 5™

Being more purposeful in your communication can take as little as five minutes. I call it "Take 5 to Communicate Well." The process involves following five simple steps that lead to better communication. With time, leaders can get so good at this smart and strategic shortcut that they can literally work through how to handle a communication strategically in just a few minutes.

OUTCOME: 1

What do you want to accomplish at the highest level? What's the business outcome you seek? Define it as specifically as you can. **WATCH OUT:** Communication is not an outcome but an enabler to reach your goals.

_____

_____

_____

_____

_____

_____

_____

AUDIENCE: 2

Who needs to be involved to achieve the desired outcome? Which individuals? Groups? The entire organization? What's their mindset on the topic you want to communicate? Then, in that context, what do you want them to think, feel and do to achieve the outcome?

_____

_____

_____

_____

_____

_____

As importantly, the messages they eventually deliver to their audiences will be better thought out and even more closely tied to the business outcomes they seek. Think about "Take **5**" as a smart shortcut and time-saver to get the results you want. With a little practice, you can internalize the five steps and increase your communication effectiveness tenfold.

TO DOWNLOAD THIS FREE TOOL, SEE PAGE 339

MESSAGES: 3

Given the audience's mindset, what are the two or three messages that will inspire the audience and move them to action? Do they need to know more about a problem or an opportunity? The information becomes the content for your message.

_____ _____ _____

_____ _____ _____

_____ _____ _____

TACTICS: 4

Consider how your audience wants to receive the message (vs. how you prefer to deliver it). The more complex the message, the "richer" the vehicle you need, meaning using a vehicle that is closest to face-to-face where you get cues and clues as to how you are communicating. Important communication should be delivered through multiple channels since repetition builds importance and trust.

_____

_____

MEASUREMENT: 5

How will you evaluate how well your message is being received? Body language or verbal response? Other feedback mechanisms? One way is by analyzing questions employees ask. If they are asking how a new situation might work, your message is getting through. If they need you to take a step back and talk more about context, you could do a better job communicating.

_____

_____

DEFINE
OUTCOMES

We spend a fair amount of time talking with our clients and leaders we work with about "desired outcomes"—the first step in planning any kind of communication. When we ask, "What's the outcome you seek?" we often get a communication goal. That's helpful to know, but communication should never be an outcome; it's a means to achieving a business outcome. When we follow-up: "What's the *business* outcome you seek?" we also often get fuzzy business goals. That said, I thought it would be valuable to define the concept of an outcome given its importance.

WITH THE OUTCOME DEFINED,

you've taken the first step in developing a communication plan that will help you achieve your goal.

The better we can define what we need to accomplish, the better the chance we will succeed at achieving it. After all, if we don't know where we're going, how will we get there? And, as was the case in *Alice in Wonderland,* "any road will get you there."

When we ask about a desired outcome, we want a business objective. That is, a measurable result like widgets sold, customers served, share of market, or people in seats. This kind of outcome is a consequence of action by teams and individuals whose goal is to deliver on the business objective.

Well defined outcomes drive smart and strategic communication planning. And while there are primary outcomes, there might also be other outcomes you want to achieve that are secondary and might be less measurable but still important, such as building a critical relationship inside an organization, getting a seat at the table, or getting promoted.

14

KNOW YOUR AUDIENCE AND THEIR NEEDS, COMMUNICATE REGULARLY

Because uncertainty and change can happen at any time, it's important to establish routines that allow for regular communication with employees. Several years ago, the company I worked for had a team that was struggling with morale. People were unhappy with their jobs. With management approval, we arranged an offsite with the Analyst base to discuss the current situation. Our group leader started the conversation by having everyone discuss one thing they liked about their job. That step led to a much more productive conversation about the things that were bothering people, and some well-considered solutions to address the challenges because we were in the right mindset to begin with. I've adopted that approach of balancing the positive with the negative as I've taken on new roles that include people management needs at other companies.

Michael Clark
is Managing
Director and
Consulting
Actuary, River
and Mercantile.

For the people I manage, there are monthly check-ins that always follow the same agenda:

1 WHAT'S GOING WELL?

2 WHAT HAS YOU SAYING, "I REALLY DON'T WANT TO GO TO WORK TODAY?"

The discussions are less about specific projects and more about how team members feel about the work they are doing. The location for these check-ins has varied, but they are regularly scheduled, and I've encouraged walking meetings, where we walk outside while having the discussion.

This approach has helped everyone keep a high-level perspective and not get bogged down in the annoyances that can creep into any job. These check-ins have also provided a forum to address problems before they become insurmountable and have allowed me to coach my direct reports on how to solve their own problems, only stepping in to run interference when necessary. In situations with change and uncertainty, there is usually a lot of negative that can be easy to focus on. Leaders who keep the focus on the big picture, the why behind all of our work, can help their teams stay far more positive, productive and satisfied in their roles.

15

TALK TO PEOPLE LIKE REAL PEOPLE

We are often schooled in business to develop a working relationship that doesn't quite cross over into a true relationship. Over the years I've moved away from that. I've learned that it's okay to be personal in the workplace, to have real conversations about your emotions or world events or the forces that shaped you as you grew up. Naturally, you have to manage performance as a leader and make tough decisions, but that gets a whole lot easier when you actually have a relationship and you're talking and coaching all the time.

At the beginning of 2020, we had a triple whammy in financial services. First, the stock market collapsed, dramatically affecting investors large and small. The Federal Reserve took action by lowering interest rates to zero, massively impacting a major revenue stream for financial services firms like ours that serve those investors. On top of this and within the space of a few short weeks, the pandemic response had basically

ground the overall economy to a halt. You can't make up for all that overnight; you need to take drastic measures and do things differently. After some stressful conversations, our leadership soon realized that we had to get out in front of everything and talk to our people directly and as people.

We began with a comprehensive employee survey and weekly all-employee calls with the CEO. Top leadership took the tough questions, including the potential for layoffs and figuring out how to manage working from home. We were candid, caring and honest, but gave the context too—what we were facing, what we had to do to pull through and thrive. And because we had established that foundation of openness and honesty starting from the CEO, we were ready to respond when the topic of racial injustice was top of mind for our employees. We tried to listen to the people whose stories we probably hadn't been asking enough about.

For instance, after a few key conversations, in particular with a couple of our leaders of color, our CEO realized he needed to lean in more. He signed a CEO pledge and brought it to the entire executive team to sign as well. Our message was that we wanted our minority team members to know that we stand with them.

From this difficult time a whole new level of dialogue has sprung. It has been great to see the walls come down in a financial services organization. In financial services, there's a tendency to cling to the process, fill in the box *"the way it's always been done."* But when these crises hit, we had a set of imperatives that were all about truthfulness and honesty, and there was nowhere to hide, no script to follow and no boxes to check.

NOWHERE TO HIDE   **NO SCRIPT TO FOLLOW**   **NO BOXES TO CHECK**

Our leadership took a bet that creating a vision for a bright future, along with transparency, honesty and timely communication, would pay off with our team sticking by us. For the most part, that's exactly what's happened. And our organization is better for it.

Jeannie Finkel
is Chief Human Resources Officer at Cetera Financial Group, based in Los Angeles. She has more than 30 years of business experience, much of it leading in financial services organizations.

194

CREATE MESSAGES THAT MATTER

In advertising and communications, effective frequency is the number of times a person must be exposed to a message before a response is made. Theories have ranged from three to 20 times, leading to countless spirited discussions amongst academics and practitioners alike looking to identify the magic number. Whatever the answer, and it varies by person, the fact remains that recipients of a message can only retain a limited amount of information per exposure and it often takes someone hearing a message multiple times to transition that person from awareness to understanding, and finally, to action.

That's why development of **clear, concise, credible** and **compelling** messages is critical to effective communications. Stopping there, however, is like ending a sentence without a period…you must be **consistent** with your messages to effectively close the loop.

Follow the *Five Cs* for successful messaging

CLEAR: Easy to understand and remember no matter the audience.

CONCISE: Direct and to the point without unnecessary insertions that may distract audiences from the main points.

CREDIBLE: Believable in that the messages are backed by proof points and incorporate supporting details to strengthen key points.

COMPELLING: Catches your audiences' attention and inspires them to take applicable action.

CONSISTENT: Repeatable and flexible enough to be incorporated into varying communication channels again and again.

To be clear, message creation is not the same as a script. There is no replacement for thoughtful, strategic core messages that are customized to your individual audience. You can have the best design or visual effects, perfect timing, and spot-on delivery, but none of that matters if your audience can't truly hear and digest them. For example, sometimes we share too much information, or information that's hard to digest, and therefore causes confusion and even anxiety. Once you have messages that meet an audience's mindset, find opportunities to weave them into different communications so employees are consistently hearing your key points in slightly different ways on a recurring basis.

The Five Cs are a critical first step, but they also need to be followed up with great core messages. Follow these steps for developing your core messages and you'll have the full picture, providing your audience with the foundational building blocks for successful communication.

IMAGINE STATEMENTS

"I ENVISION...

Those two words carry with them huge potential—for you, your employees, and for the results you want to achieve. It's about your aspirations, dreams, and the exciting future you envision. One of the most critical skills of best-in-class leaders is an ability to paint a picture of the future. It's not just any future but one that each of us can envision, one

be part of the journey. These "dreams" often start with the words "imagine" or "what if?" This is simply about stating your business goal and then talking about what's possible. Employees want to be engaged in a meaningful journey toward a worthy destination. That dream sets the context and playing field and describes where you're headed.

WHAT MAKES A GOOD
"imagine" statement?

IT SHOULD:

TIE to your goals and describe a compelling image of what's possible

APPEAL to others to share in the future you envision

DESCRIBE an inspirational future that people want to be a part of and therefore will work hard to help get you there

Change the way you talk about things:

You often can resolve a negative situation by changing the context and your delivery:

- Think about the way you have been talking about a major initiative or project. Is it hopeful? Filled with energy? Cautious? Fearful?
- Are you celebrating the early wins and successes?

If your approach to discussing business results leaves people feeling less than enthused, change your approach to a team-inspiring one, and watch the results change.

Best cadence and rhythm in times of crisis:

- Big picture: The best leaders already have a regular cadence and rhythm for communicating with key stakeholders.
- A communications cadence is often defined through a communications calendar of regularly scheduled touch points with various audiences that are important to you.
- During uncertain times like this, it's important to add many more touch points to that calendar, and allow for many more opportunities for dialogue.

Remember to consider how your audiences are working:

- Who is remote?
- Who is on-site (at a plant, hospital, store, in the field, etc.)?
- Who is rotating between the two depending on the day or week?

16

EMPLOY YOUR LEARNINGS, EMBRACE THE DIFFERENCES

After being a part of the higher education sector for the past 15 years, I have seen thousands of broad informational emails that are sent to the entire university population meant to inform our constituents on any number of topics. If the goal was to push news, then we did our job. But if the ultimate goal is to actually engage and inspire, we need to do more to fully understand and address the diverse needs of our constituency. In my current role, I work with a network of 300,000+ alumni worldwide. As you can imagine, the wants and needs of these constituents varies widely. One message generates a wide variety of reactions and emotions. So how do we engage broad and diverse people in ways that feel

meaningful? This process began for me with my first trip to Shanghai in 2013, where I met a group of alumni that was very candid. They opened my eyes to the opportunities we are missing by trying to create a one-size-fits-all communication plan. This became even more clear when the pandemic significantly affected the United States in March and I needed to reimagine how I connect to our community without travel and in-person connections. With a global audience, I knew that the spread and mitigation of the virus was different across countries and communities. I looked at what programs we could postpone or cancel this year that relied heavily on volunteer support through our alumni network.

We met virtually with alumni to ask what would be useful during this time. Was it connecting socially, learning new skills, or mentoring a recent graduate? In asking questions, we learned the needs of our alumni and formed closer bonds to our volunteers by encouraging them to express their ideas and even frustrations. By creating new engagement opportunities and new communication pathways based on what we heard, we found approaches that will last long after the pandemic. In particular, our focus with our communications for alumni groups located outside of the U.S. are much more in-depth and detail oriented.

We have seen that during this move to a virtual world, time and resources were actually strained more than ever as areas felt the need to push out as much content as possible. It's great to see a change in the mindset that more isn't always better, and that it's best to focus on actual outcomes. The lessons I learned have and will continue to shape the way that I engage with our alumni.

"
MORE
ISN'T ALWAYS
BETTER

Never again will the phrase "We always do it this way" be part of our communication plan. We need to hold on to the agility we exhibited and capitalize on how much less threatening new technologies are. Perhaps most importantly, I've learned to listen intently first and respond in more personalized ways.

THE CHANGE MAKERS

Jason Kane is Director of Constituent Relations for the University of Pittsburgh. In this role, he is responsible for engaging alumni from around the world and increasing the global footprint of the university. He brings more than 10 years' experience in advancement, donor and alumni services to the challenge of forming a network of international alumni who support Pitt's global vision and strategy.

17

RECOGNIZE YOUR "BUMPER CAR MOMENTS" AND TURN CHALLENGES INTO OPPORTUNITIES

When a change is dramatic and tumultuous, it's important to consider how individuals in an organization might need to heal. For that healing to begin, leaders need to first consider their own level of well-being and need for personal growth. While this process should always be done, times of change afford leaders the chance for self-examination and monitoring of the long-held paradigms that might be impacting their responses and style.

A leader needs to watch themselves for repeated trends in their own behavior and discover their own "bumper car moments." These "bumper car moments" are when normal workplace conflicts—such as getting passed for a promotion or a disapproving boss—collide with the deeply ingrained childhood past and self-limiting beliefs. When they collide, old strategies kick in. These moments also include times of change. For example, the leader who focuses on perfectionism is likely reacting out of past feelings of inadequacy or somehow believing they are "less than" with a sense they need to constantly prove themselves to others. By seeing the pattern, a leader can consider new options for actions and reactions during moments of conflict at work. When this happens, the leader is more able to lead change. The less we spend in reaction or being emotionally triggered at work, and especially during change, the more able leaders are to lead others through transformation. The new response comes down to reframing the questions we ask ourselves and having a full recognition that we have choices in our next steps. It really can be as simple as saying what's going right, rather than what's going wrong. When a leader asks themselves or the organization the "right" question, the energy in the room shifts. It's almost like a switch is flipped and the lights come on.

A leader has the power to ignite new thinking that shifts what might first be perceived as a problem to an opportunity for innovative approaches and new insights. Never underestimate the influence of leadership. When a leader first discerns what drives their own behaviors, an example for others is set. And, the impact is not limited to the organization's employees; it can easily extend to the employees' families and others who witness the spirit and shift of focus to a positive one. This kind of self-reflective leadership creates resilience and an organization that is much more likely to see the opportunities of change.

"NEVER UNDERESTIMATE THE INFLUENCE OF LEADERSHIP.

Susan Schmitt Winchester is Chief HR Officer at Applied Materials, a materials engineering technology company. She previously served as Senior Vice President of Human Resources for Rockwell Automation. Her innovative mindset and commitment to excellence define her leadership style. She continually looks to meet today's global business challenges with creative HR strategies that engage people, enable exceptional performance and support a dynamic, inclusive corporate culture. Susan is the author of *Healing at Work: A Guide to Using Career Conflicts to Overcome Your Past and Build the Future You Deserve*, with co-author Martha Finney.

COMMUNICATION CADENCE

ENHANCE EMPLOYEE ENGAGEMENT AND DRIVE PERFORMANCE USING THESE SIMPLE STEPS

PLAN: Identify relevant stakeholder audience(s): _____

HOW: Determine how best to reach them:

- ☐ One-on-one meeting
- ☐ Team meeting/virtual call
- ☐ Department meeting
- ☐ Town hall meeting
- ☐ Walk the halls/rounds
- ☐ Email update
- ☐ Social media
- ☐ Blog post
- ☐ Digital signage
- ☐ Other: _____

FREQUENCY: How often:

- ☐ Daily
- ☐ Once a week
- ☐ Once a month
- ☐ Twice a month
- ☐ Once a quarter
- ☐ Twice a quarter
- ☐ Other: _____

PLOT: Establish your cadence and plot the touchpoint(s) on your calendars.

 TO DOWNLOAD THIS FREE TOOL, SEE PAGE 339

TIPS

Here are some touch points to consider for each audience:
Focus on high-visibility and high-frequency communications...

During times of crisis, check in daily, if not more often. Otherwise, check-in regularly. Make a point to "see" and dialogue with every person on your team. Ensure that you are showing employees that you see them, hear them, and that they matter.

Be "visible" even when teams are remote. Pick up the phone, use video conferencing or other social media platforms to shoot a quick instant message, etc.

Hold daily 10-minute huddles on MS Teams/Skype/ WebEx/Zoom so people can see each other and feel connected and go over the game plan for the day. At key times, it is a much more valuable experience to see one another than to be on a conference call.

Hold smaller group meetings with groups that have similar concerns. Think micro so you're giving more people a chance to engage. Instead of a town hall, do a mini-town hall with all people leaders, or all shift leaders at a manufacturing plant.

Finally, make sure all of your people leaders have a cadence with the appropriate touch points with their audiences.

Q&A:

Frequently asked questions on dialogue and cadence

Q:

What is the right amount of communication? How do I know, as I think about my communications cadence, that it's enough (not too much or too little)?

A:

One of the best ways to know is to ask. It could be in a conversation with all your direct reports, or in a one-on-one with each of your team members, or both. Give folks a continuum of "exactly the right amount—too much—not enough" and ask them to help you with where your communication lands on the continuum and why.

I also suggest asking your team what's working today that you should continue with, and if they have ideas for improving the cadence. In general, research I saw about communication during COVID-19 shows employees wanted and needed to hear from their leaders a lot. It's almost impossible to overcommunicate during a time of crisis.

Q:

I wanted to get more dialogue with an "all hands" style meeting and it wasn't getting much traction. How would you recommend handling video communications with my team?

A:

I recommend trying some small-group video conferences. Think "micro." Gathering smaller groups in this format can help create an environment where people feel more comfortable opening up. The town hall is still an important vehicle in your cadence, and I suggest adding some of the small group virtual meetings in, too. The meetings provide an opportunity for you to continue listening, and proactively give folks comfort and understanding—and a different way to connect with you.

CHAPTER 6

FRAME THE CONTEXT AND MAKE IT RELEVANT

Once you have a plan for your communications and a cadence that's all your own, the next important thing to tackle is your approach to maximizing every **individual** communication. Context is key, along with making your messages super relevant to employees. Context is critical because it tells your employees what importance to place on something, what assumptions to draw (or not) about what is being communicated, and most importantly, the ultimate meaning to the message. Relevance is about answering the top question on many employees' minds: *What's in it for me?*

CON-TEXT [KON-TEKST] *n.* **NOUN**

1. *The parts of a written or spoken statement that precede or follow a specific word or passage, usually influencing its meaning or effect*

2. *The set of circumstances or facts that surround a particular event, situation, etc.*

WHY CONTEXT IS THE KEY

To obtain alignment, focus on context first

At the heart of organization-wide alignment is a common context. Context influences how we interpret information. It's the lens through which we view and make sense of the world. Think about context like a map at a large airport. To understand where you are, you need a map of the layout—that's the big picture, the context. From there you can determine where you need to go and how to get there.

Each of us comes to the workplace with our own context because of how we're raised, our experience, background, and so on. That's a wonderful thing because we need diversity more than ever today. Yet context influences how we interpret information. It's the lens through which we view and make sense of the world around us. As leaders, part of our role is to create a shared organizational context, as opposed to an individual's context. You achieve that when you connect the dots between what you say and what your employees already know by setting context in terms of where your listener is coming from:

Explaining the "why" behind a plan or changes, which might include topics such as current results, customer requirements, competitive data, market opportunities, and more. Then explaining the "what," "how," "who" and "when"

Making it relevant, by answering the question (or helping employees answer the question for themselves): "What's in it for me?" Once employees know that, they understand how they fit in and contribute.

5 Ws AND AN H

A tool to communicate virtually anything

Ask any journalist and they will tell you any solid news story covers the following six concepts: *Why*, *What*, *Where*, *When*, *Who* and *How*. The same is true for communicating inside an organization, especially in uncertain or challenging times. By addressing the 5 Ws and an H, you can ensure you capture important perspective, share the all-important context, and make the information relevant for your audience.

The principle behind the 5 Ws and an H is that each question should be answered with the facts necessary for the story to be complete. None of these questions can be answered with a simple "yes" or "no." They require context and detail so the information is meaningful and relevant and answers the main questions on everyone's minds.

WHY:

Thinking has evolved on where to begin with the 5 Ws and an H. Among the latest ideas is one from noted management consultant Simon Sinek which is to begin with **why** as it tends to reach an emotional chord with audiences that can inspire the actions you desire. He suggests that the most forward-thinking organizations start with the conceptual and go to the specific. So, particularly when communicating about vision, values and broad concepts, start with the **why**.

ANSWER:

- Why is it the right decision?
- Why now?
- Why is it important?

WHAT:

Feeling inspired, people have a strong desire to know more about the **what**. When your messages are more concrete and process oriented, you might even consider beginning with the **what**. In either case, this "w" serves as the foundation on which your information is built and can set a strong roadmap to guide your actions.

ANSWER:

- What's the decision?
- What does it mean?
- What do employees need to know and understand?
- What's in it for me, the employee?

WHO:

The **who** sometimes seems simple. But, rather than taking broad strokes to describe all those involved and your stakeholders with phrases like "leaders" or "all employees," think about the breakdown of the larger groups as you pose your questions. For example, your messages to hourly employees or those working virtually would likely be different than mid-level managers. And, be mindful to think cross functionally and avoid department silos.

ANSWER:

- Who made the decision?
- Who's in charge?
- Who does it impact?

5 Ws AND AN H

(continued)

WHERE:

Like the who, the where needs a thoughtful, detailed analysis for your efforts to be most successful. This is particularly true for large multinational organizations when the **where** might be quite variable. The important role technology can play in facilitating communications across organizations also needs to be a part of your exploration of the **where**.

ANSWER:

- Where is this decision coming from?
- Where/what locations will it affect?
- Where can employees get more information?

WHEN:

To meet your deadlines and know how to effectively cascade your messages, the **when**—often in the form of a communications plan—can provide a sense of direction and sometimes urgency. The **when** is sometimes influenced by competing factors. It's important to stay attuned to conflicting priorities and be ready to "push back" if necessary when the impact of your communications efforts could be diminished by unrealistic timelines.

ANSWER:

- When are all these decisions and changes happening?
- What specific milestone events are being planned?

HOW:

It may be last on this list, but the **how** should hardly be considered the least. The **how** is usually the "work horse" of your planning team and guides your project planning with tasks and tactics. It's also the place where discussion and even debate of ideas should be plentiful.

ANSWER:

- How was the decision made?
- How will it be implemented?
- How will communications flow internally and externally?
- How does it impact employees?

REMEMBER:

One of the best ways to ensure you're providing great context for employees is to tell a complete story, addressing *ALL* these key questions.

TO DOWNLOAD THIS FREE TOOL, SEE PAGE 339

18

THE RIGHT SENSE OF PURPOSE HELPS TRANSFORMATIONS SUCCEED

As Chief Transformation Officer at TreeHouse Foods, I help drive new capabilities and improved leverage of our shared resources across the organization. As a private-label food company, almost everything we do in some way is custom for our customers' brands, so it's important that we continue to find new ways to become more efficient and effective. One of the biggest challenges we have had this year is that consumers have dramatically changed their behaviors with food because of the pandemic. Many more of us are eating at home, driving at-home consumption levels way up. This change happened almost overnight at the onset of the pandemic and

continues at elevated rates, requiring our employees to rise to the challenge of meeting the unexpected increase in demand. Employee health and safety has also been our highest priority. Our folks are essential workers in food manufacturing plants and keeping them safe and healthy is always at the forefront of everything we do.

To manage change in this kind of environment, we first had to acknowledge the reality of the situation, at the market level, the corporate level, and at a personal level. Employees want leaders who understand how a crisis is impacting not just the business, but its people. The second foundational part to

> **EMPLOYEES WANT LEADERS WHO UNDERSTAND HOW A CRISIS IS IMPACTING NOT JUST THE BUSINESS, BUT ITS PEOPLE.**

leading through change is communicating a clear strategy to manage the crisis, mapping out your plans for how you'll get to the other side—and sharing what that means for individuals. People need to know how they can contribute, what they can do, and what their purpose is. I can't underscore enough how important that sense of purpose is when you're driving change, whether there is a crisis or not. When people are purpose driven, they know how to navigate challenges because they have a guiding star and understand where they're trying to land. With that, they bring their best self to work because the benefit is larger than them or the business. The purpose needs to land far beyond the dollars, to show how you intend to have some sort of lasting impact. When you have that, it makes people more creative, more dedicated, and more resilient.

At TreeHouse, our purpose is making high quality food and beverages affordable to all. That purpose has become even more relevant as we manage through the pandemic, and I know it's inspiring to our employees. Inside our company, we always want to reinforce that message. We want to be great partners to our customers, delivering on their product needs. But right now, we also want to provide a little comfort in the midst of this difficult time by ensuring that our friends and families and neighbors will find the groceries and value they need at the store. With that purpose in mind, every change we make gets defined in that context, and becomes easier to embrace.

THE CHANGE MAKERS

Triona Schmelter is Senior Vice President and Chief Transformation Officer of TreeHouse Foods. She has more than 20 years of experience in the food industry, holding a variety of leadership roles at Kraft and General Mills. Triona is also a member of the Board of Directors of Steelcase, Inc., a leading furniture manufacturer.

19

FOCUS ON THE UPSIDES OF CHANGE AND GROWTH

I love driving transformations and helping companies execute new strategies. One of the biggest transformations I've been involved with happened early in my career, when National City Mortgage (now PNC Mortgage) reduced its 93 operation branches across the United States to just three, in very short order. It was intense, and really difficult, but I learned so much from that experience that shaped how I lead through change today.

One of the biggest insights from that experience is my belief in the power of seeing the positives in change. That involves painting a picture of the future and telling stories of what success looks like. With the transformation that I'm leading now at PeopleReady, I am always reminding people why we're here and how we'll make a difference for the company. When people are rallying around an end goal, it helps them more easily work through the change. If you're not able to bring people along through change, you

see "black holes" occur, where people either actively or inactively disagree with the change initiative. Sometimes the inactive ones — the silent objectors — are some of the toughest to manage, so they're especially important to identify and bring along.

One of the other keys to driving change as a leader is identifying your strengths. What I've learned about myself is that I like to focus on achieving something every day, so I really lean into this when I'm driving organizational change. Personally, I try to set three goals each day of things I want to accomplish. At the end of the day, I look back and say, "Did I accomplish those three?" I encourage my team members to do the same. Some days, you might feel terrible because you weren't able to achieve much against your goals. But over time, when you start to add up all the little wins, you see that they slowly turn into much bigger wins — and therefore, you're helping create steady change for the organization. This idea of managing to your "top three" of the day is extremely important during intense times of change, like the pandemic. In times like that, it's natural for people to become easily distracted.

But when you focus only on your top three goals every day, you can have accomplishments and successes each and every day. At many large organizations like the ones I've worked at throughout my career, there are so many competing priorities, which makes it hard for individual employees to focus and even harder for people to feel like they can have an impact. When I conduct all-hands meetings, I frequently say, "This is where we need to focus right now. Here are your priorities for this month."

It makes such a difference because then everyone is focusing on the most important things. I also encourage team members to block time in their workday to focus on their top three priorities. That's the time to stop looking at the emails, shut off Teams, and make a

point to spend time on the most impactful priorities, rather than getting distracted by thousands of other things.

Finally, in managing through change, I think it's helpful to have team members focus on all the skills they're acquiring. During the annual performance review as well as quarterly check ins, I spend a lot of time with my team members walking them through the new things they've learned, particularly in a challenging moment or year like the one we've just lived through. When employees start to see just how much they're learning and growing, they come to value their experience even more.

Also, the accountability is really important for people to succeed. I feel you need to hold people accountable for their own growth, while also being supportive along the way. That's where reflection is critically important: What am I going to repeat tomorrow? What am I going to do better tomorrow? No matter the task or challenge, you're taking the time to focus on you—and you're learning even more how to grow.

Denise Sparacio is Senior Director of the Program Management Office for PeopleReady, a national staffing agency. Denise is a seasoned change management project leader. She has previously served as Global Director of Commercial Strategy for GE Healthcare, Director of the Program Management Office at Redbox/Outerwall, and Vice President of the Project Management Office for PNC Mortgage, among other roles.

**CONTEXT
EMPLOYEES
HAVE**

**CONTEXT
LEADERS
"THINK"
EMPLOYEES
HAVE**

CONTEXT IN UNCERTAIN TIMES

Based on what's happening in the moment, the context you
provide may need to continually fluctuate. This may seem
like a simple concept, but one of the biggest mistakes
leaders make is they forget to communicate the WHY.

TRAP: *"They already know it"*

It's human nature to think others have the same information leaders have, so we skip critical details that provide context. It's like a story where you're on Chapter 14, and your staff are on various beginning chapters. It's natural to forget they haven't been privy to the discussions that leadership has, and therefore we need to start communication with Chapter One. That context is critically important, even if some have heard it before. Think about it as "Once Upon A Time" in headline form—set up the situation and show the big picture so everyone starts with the same base of knowledge.

Relevance/what's in it for me?

In setting the context for employees, it's important to answer one of the biggest questions always on employees' minds: What's in it for me? Especially in a crisis situation, people have little patience for hearing about topics they don't see as directly meaningful to them, things that may be seen like distractions from getting their work done on deadline or under pressure. Serious times call for focus on serious issues. As a leader, you need to filter out what really doesn't matter today and focus on what does.

Let go of any need for approval

When communicating in a time of uncertainty or change, the goal isn't that everyone is going to like the decisions you make as a leader. They simply aren't always going to like what's happening inside the organization or in the world, no matter what you say or how you say it. As leaders, we can't change the reality. But we can help people understand and grow to accept it. Here are two main ways for helping employees reach that level of understanding and acceptance:

KEEP IN MIND:

Fully explain the rationale behind the decision, then discuss a company value or key principle that guided it.

For example, your desire to keep people safe, ensure the long-term health of the business, be as equitable as possible to everyone, protect the community, etc.

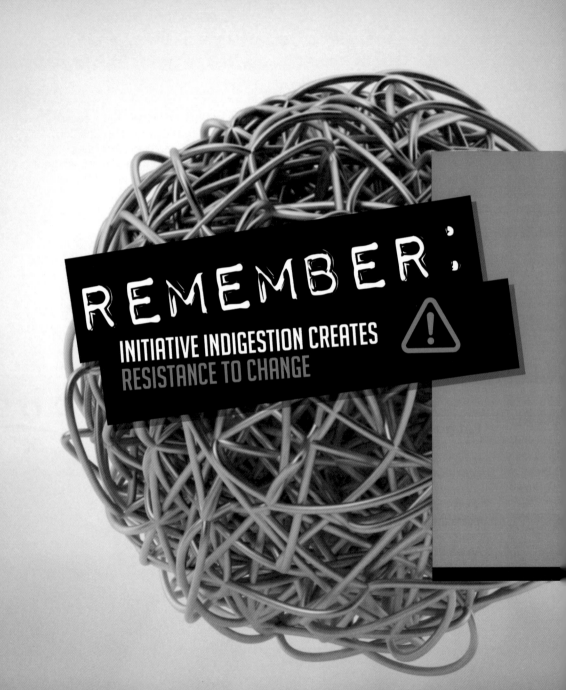

REMEMBER:
INITIATIVE INDIGESTION CREATES
RESISTANCE TO CHANGE

We all know that change is part of business and isn't going away any time soon. Employees are bombarded with so much information of all kinds that they can't digest it. That's why it's so important to place change in context to help employees adjust.

THINK
ahead and draw clear linkages between the initiative and the business imperative driving the change—be sure to explain the "whats" as well as the "whys."

PAINT
a picture of what the change means to them and spend time thinking about how they might react to that change.

CREATE
your own calendar of communication events and milestones to ensure you keep people in the loop along the way.

20

TO TRULY LEAD, TAKE ACTION AND BE PART OF THE SOLUTION

With the many challenges facing businesses today, leaders need to set an expectation that they are willing to have tough conversations. That is a first and critical step. Leaders need to be authentic, as their customers and teams can tell if they are truly committed to being part of the solution. When we lean in to the issues or the discomfort, we can better understand people's challenges—both professionally and personally—which better positions us to lead through times of significant change.

When trying to solve complex challenges, I believe it's important to start with the end in mind. We have to be honest about the current state of affairs, talk about where we are headed, and how we expect to achieve our goals, using both traditional hard skills as well as soft skills.

I've learned that leaders need to step up, step in and not wait hoping the crisis will pass. This requires leaders to be solutions-oriented. What is the measurable progress you expect to achieve? It's not just discussing the challenges but explaining what actions you are taking, and how everyone can be part of the solution. The process of change starts with awareness, but quickly moves into the action phase, with outlines of the tangible steps the team will take together.

Further, I've learned that the best leaders constantly ask themselves the big-picture questions, such as what is my "why," the thing that motivates me every morning to get up and make a difference.

For me, it's always been simple, broken down into four basic principles that guide my approach to leadership:

 Serving our communities and helping people in their times of need.

 Being a lifelong learner; always embracing opportunities to learn something new.

 Solving complex issues by embracing being part of the solution.

 Going into leadership with a sense of responsibility to leave the organization better than I found it, to make a positive mark on the culture and the long-term vision.

Personally, it is about measuring myself against the progress I am making in each of the four areas listed above. Likewise, leadership is about continually finding ways to evolve and be more effective. I just want to keep reminding myself that every day presents me with an opportunity to make an impact.

THE CHANGE MAKERS

Kurt Small is Senior Vice President and Chief Operating Officer of the Government Business Division for Anthem, Inc., a leading healthcare benefits company. In this role, he is responsible for the operational and technology strategies which drive growth and competitiveness across the Government Business Division. Under his leadership, the organization serves roughly 11 million Medicare and Medicaid members stretching across 23 states.

CHAPTER 7

TALK OPENLY ABOUT WHAT'S HAPPENING

One of the biggest traps leaders fall into is waiting to communicate, thinking they need more time to gather more facts or additional clarity and context. This tendency holds leaders back even more today when there's been so much change and uncertainty, making it nearly impossible to keep up with everything that's happening.

The information vacuum

While you're waiting to communicate, there's what I call the information vacuum that fills up whether you want it to or not. Said another way, while you're waiting, the grapevine is communicating for you, and most often perpetuating misinformation and myths, which then forces you to handle the clean up. A better strategy is to communicate proactively. For most of us, that means not waiting—using one of our planned touch points as a cadence. And if it's more time-sensitive, you can do a separate add-on communication. Chances are there's more leaders know that would be valuable to employees than they might think, which merits a communication touch point.

What happens when we wait to communicate about change?

Confusion

Miscommunication

Disengagement

More work/perception of more work

Rumor mill/grapevine

4 MAIN PROBLEMS
that come with poor communication:

1
LACK OF KNOWING

When people don't have the information they feel they need, low productivity results. People tend to avoid situations in which they will be seen as not knowing or not having expertise. No one wants to look like they don't know what to do. Think back to school; how many times did you hear teachers and professors say, "There's no such thing as a dumb question?" They knew someone had a question—a very good question that would help shed new light on the conversation—that they were simply too afraid to ask.

2
LOW MORALE

Employees want to be engaged so they feel connected to the organization. When they are, they are willing to work harder, smarter, and be active in the workplace in ways that drive business results. When they aren't engaged, they suffer. This might seem like a touchy-feely, soft business issue, but unhappy and disconnected employees can have a profound effect on business through absenteeism, lack of motivation and turnover.

3
BAD INTERPERSONAL RELATIONSHIPS

How often do you see eyes roll? How much muttering do you quietly hear? When people don't feel connected to each other, it opens up the door for misinterpretation, and for questioning motives and intent. The lack of feeling respected or listened to—truly listened to—leads people to feel negated. When that happens, they often find ways to "push back," even when they can't do it openly or directly.

4
THE "GRAPEVINE EFFECT"

Marvin Gaye isn't the only one who's heard it through the grapevine. No matter how much you might love his Motown hit, you don't want one of these growing in your organization. Yet, by not sharing information, you are ensuring a grapevine will sprout—causing problems and distractions. If you aren't talking proactively about issues that are important to your employees, chances are that someone else is—regardless of the accuracy and truthfulness of their "information."

So if there are all these downsides, why aren't we communicating better?

It's not as if management comes to work each day saying, "I want to withhold information." Likewise, employees don't say, "I want to screw something up!" So, what's at play? In many cases, it starts with our beliefs about communication that get in the way. Holding us back from greatness are beliefs and fear.

• We believe we are born good at communicating and therefore don't practice and don't get better

• We're afraid of failing, and that fear stops us from trying and learning new things or skills

• We have a mistaken belief that good communication is all "common sense"

• We inaccurately assume others know what we know

To really address the downsides of poor communication, to get to the many upsides of effective communication and accelerate our business results, we have to examine our beliefs and, in some cases, change them. Improving communication involves more than just disseminating the message properly so that it's heard (though that alone can be a challenge). It means ensuring that the message resonates with and is understood by the listener(s) in a way that will move them to action. It's hard work, but it's worth it.

The three wants employees have

Earlier in the book, we talked about employee needs and *The Eight Key Questions All Employees Have (see page 125)*. We also talked broadly about their wants. That said, what do most employees really want in times of change? Answers to these three points:

• What their leaders know, when they know it

• What their leaders don't know

• Information presented in a truthful way

THINK OF IT AS 3+1
when communicating

**HERE'S
WHAT WE
KNOW**

**HERE'S
WHAT WE
DON'T
KNOW**

**HERE'S
WHAT WE'RE
WORKING ON
FINDING
OUT**

**PROACTIVELY
BUST
MYTHS**

For example,
you might say:
*"I want to address
something I heard
that's not true"*—
and then share
exactly what it is
you know and what
you don't know.
Busting myths is
a critical step that
leaders must do
proactively, but
often miss.

COMMUNICATE IN TIMES OF CHANGE

It can be frustrating for leaders to recognize they don't have all the answers. It makes you feel like things are just happening to you, and that nothing is truly in your control. But you can take comfort in the fact that employees don't expect you to have all the answers. In fact, they probably wouldn't trust you if you said you had all the answers! Instead, employees just want to know what you do know and when you know it (without unnecessary delays in relaying the communication). And, they want you to share in a truthful, authentic way.

WHAT YOU KNOW:

_____

_____

_____

WHAT YOU DON'T KNOW:

_____

_____

_____

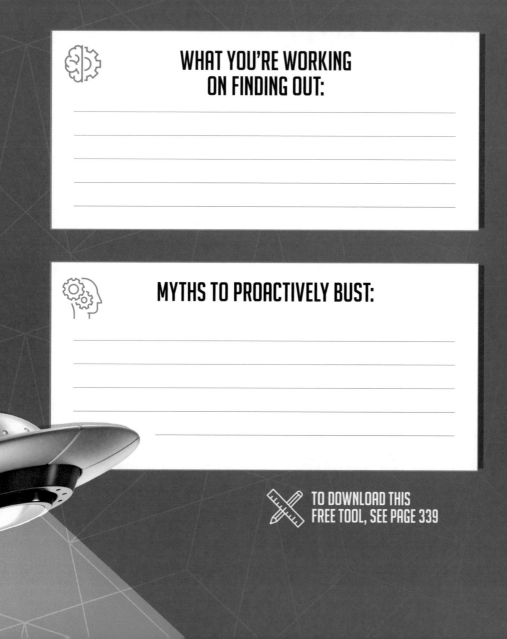

**WHAT YOU'RE WORKING
ON FINDING OUT:**

MYTHS TO PROACTIVELY BUST:

TO DOWNLOAD THIS
FREE TOOL, SEE PAGE 339

WHY PEOPLE RESIST CHANGE

A colleague of mine, Les Landes, shared the following wisdom with me recently. See how you might fill in this blank:

It's not that people resist change. People resist_____.

There's a myriad of answers to the question, but the themes often overlap. People resist change without their involvement, they don't like change forced down their throats. People naturally resist being controlled and being uninvolved in decisions that affect them. The most effective change communications (whenever possible) is a collaborative process, not a top-down effort. It involves team members in conversations regarding change where people can feel some control over what's happening.

Tell me, and I will forget. Show me, and I may remember. Involve me, and I will understand.

— CONFUCIUS

The success equation for helping people hear you

It's human nature to read into another person's actions—to attach meaning to it, which is often based on ourselves and how we see the world. That's the cause of a lot of miscommunication in the workplace.

To help others hear us, it's critical we share our motivation and intent. Others can't know our motivation or intent—they can only guess at it, and have more than a 50/50 chance of being wrong. More often than we'd like, they'll attach a meaning we don't intend. The other piece of this success equation is to talk about our motivation and intent in a way that benefits the audience: Your employees. They need to understand that what we're sharing is in their best interest to hear, and why.

The benefits of describing motivation and intent

Add one of these two phrases to your leader toolkit:

1) My motivation here is…(benefit to the other person)

2) My intent in sharing this with you is…(benefit to the other person)

"My motivation here is to help you increase your presence in front of senior leadership."

WHAT THIS MIGHT SOUND LIKE

"My intent in sharing this is to help you develop and become a VP, which I know is a goal of yours."

Sharing your motivation and intent help you do an even better job communicating with employees, and doing it in a way that perks the audience up and makes them want to listen.

234

21

EMBRACE BRAVE CONVERSATIONS

As the Senior Director of Inclusion and Diversity at Baxter International Inc., I'm highly committed to enhancing our corporate culture. And while it has been clear for some time that more candid and authentic conversations need to happen inside corporations today, the events of the past year certainly underscore the point.

The corporate paradigm about what can and can't be discussed clearly needs to take a dramatic shift. I believe this shift starts with leaders allowing themselves to be vulnerable and telling their own stories first. Likewise, leaders need to gain a comfort level with challenging, even troubling conversations, including dialogue that explores the day-to-day lives of individual employees from diverse communities. The conventional small talk, "how was your weekend?" type chats should be replaced with a much deeper examination of what's really happening with people. For instance, until we hear firsthand from a Black male professional how he was stopped by police and questioned on his way to a corporate meeting, it can be difficult to comprehend that life experience. Because of this, I believe becoming an empathetic listener is going to be a fundamental leadership skill going forward. A dedication to equipping managers to build this new expertise should be a priority for all organizations.

For some time, corporate efforts on diversity have been described as creating "safe spaces," but a better description is probably "brave spaces"—bravery from the perspective of having both leaders and employees sharing a mutual awareness that experiences might be different, but that common ground can be uncovered.

While listening is essential, I also firmly believe that it's no longer enough to listen. Instead, honest, authentic discussions should take us to a different place—to real action. Leaders should apply the newfound knowledge we gather to regularly revisit the effectiveness of the actions we take. Leaders who embrace honesty and have an ongoing willingness to change again if needed will be far more effective leading on the critical needs surrounding inclusion and diversity.

Lisa Keltner
is Senior Director, Inclusion & Diversity at Baxter International Inc., Lisa is responsible for the company's global inclusion and diversity (I&D) strategy, including the coordination and management of the company's Global Inclusion Council and Business Resource Groups. She also partners with the Talent Acquisition and Talent Management teams to develop and execute strategies to attract, retain, develop and engage diverse talent.

22

ILLUSTRATING STABILITY, ALIGNING WORDS AND ACTIONS

Change management theory suggests that in times of personal or organizational flux, it is important to find things that are not changing. Finding sources of stability therefore can be an anchor in a tidal wave of disruption. Communicating messages to employees that reflect a firm foundation and resilience is key to keeping an organization moving forward, especially when human tendencies may lead us to believe we are "stuck," or worse, things are "out of control." To make this possible, leaders need to spend considerable time planning early and evaluating "worst-case" and "best-case" scenarios with honesty and integrity. Your team will

recognize quickly if your "worst-case" scenario, is in fact, not the worst-case. Likewise, a redoubling of efforts to ensure that internal audiences learn any organizational news directly from the leadership, rather than hear/read about something via media reports, or external sources (i.e., other customers, vendors) is critical. Messaging needs to remain consistent and frequent, with continual assessments of how information shared is being heard. This requires listening to your team immediately following announcements. In times of disruptive change, there is no "one size fits all" so leaders need to be ready to adjust course if needed. Keeping a frequent pulse of

what works and what doesn't is required, as such times of change often represent a great opportunity for companies to analyze and improve their operations and processes. Understanding change as it occurs also allows strong companies to capture valuable learning lessons during times of uncertainty. While it's always important when conditions are uncertain, following through on what is communicated and promised is vital. Even the most well-crafted message will be discredited if employees identify a disconnect.

REMEMBER:
In times of change, there is increased scrutiny on what leaders say and what leaders do. Laser focus attention from leaders needs to ensure that words and actions always align.

Bradley A. Feuling is the Chairman and Chief Executive Officer of The Asia Institute/ Kong and Allan Group. Feuling works closely with the leadership team on the strategic advancement of the organization, while also heading up the U.S. office based in Austin, Texas.

TRUST AS A POWERFUL TOOL

Jumping off a high dive. Getting behind the wheel for the first time. Giving your first speech in front of a large crowd. When you look back at some of the scariest things you've done in life, chances are a big reason you achieved them was trust. Maybe a parent was standing by your side to assure you a plunge from that sky-high diving board would actually be good for you, that you'd be ok, and that you had their support. In other cases, it may have been a friend, a spouse or a colleague guiding you and encouraging you. The trust you had in that person gave you the courage needed to take a leap, or simply follow their lead.

Trust is a major driver for all of us, and sadly, it's in short supply today. The *2021 Edelman Trust Barometer*, the annual worldwide trust and credibility survey, found public trust in government, non-governmental institutions and the media had eroded even further over the past year. More than half of global respondents said that they felt government and business leaders are deliberately misleading with lies and misinformation.

Trust in business is higher than other institutions

However, there was a bright spot for business leaders. The study found that most people now rely mostly on their employers for accurate information, and trust businesses over government and media. It's noteworthy that employees specifically called out their own companies as a major source of trusted information. *(Nudge for communicators: Here's evidence that internal communications truly matters!)*

Interestingly, respondents were also looking for more from their CEOs. More than 8 in 10 respondents expect CEOs to publicly speak out on societal challenges like the impact of the pandemic, job automation and local community issues; 68 percent want CEOs to step in when government won't fix societal problems; and 65 percent want CEOs to hold themselves as accountable to the public as to shareholders. Here's a snapshot of how businesses currently lead other institutions when it comes to trust and the information they provide:

Percent trust in:

76%	61%	57%	53%	51%
MY EMPLOYER	BUSINESS (GENERAL)	NON-GOVERNMENTAL ORGANIZATIONS	GOVERNMENT	MEDIA

Percent who believe information from each source automatically, or after seeing it twice or less:

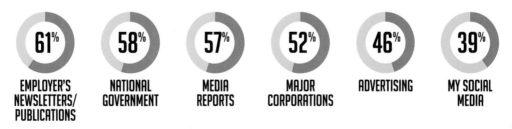

61%	58%	57%	52%	46%	39%
EMPLOYER'S NEWSLETTERS/ PUBLICATIONS	NATIONAL GOVERNMENT	MEDIA REPORTS	MAJOR CORPORATIONS	ADVERTISING	MY SOCIAL MEDIA

Expressing disagreement without being disagreeable

When you need to provide criticism to team members in an open and honest way, begin by acknowledging the positive points. Then, be specific about what you disagree with. You want your colleague to be open and hear your thoughts, not be defensive. A free exchange of ideas will lead to the best outcome. To keep the dialogue open, here are some tips to keep in mind:

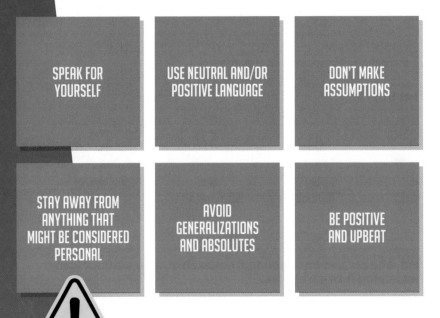

SPEAK FOR YOURSELF

USE NEUTRAL AND/OR POSITIVE LANGUAGE

DON'T MAKE ASSUMPTIONS

STAY AWAY FROM ANYTHING THAT MIGHT BE CONSIDERED PERSONAL

AVOID GENERALIZATIONS AND ABSOLUTES

BE POSITIVE AND UPBEAT

Avoid going to extremes

When you're sharing constructive criticism or coaching employees, avoid extremes like *always*, *never*, and *worst*. Sweeping generalizations like these can trigger a defensive posture. It's better to be as objective and accurate as you can be in describing the situation.

MATCH WORDS AND ACTIONS

Building trust and credibility is about ensuring your words match your actions.
How do your words link up with your actions?

WHAT I'M SAYING:	GAPS:	WHAT I'M DOING:

Now ask others: What do you hear me saying consistently?
What do you see me doing consistently?

WHAT OTHERS SAY I SAY:	GAPS:	WHAT OTHERS SEE ME DO:

**TO DOWNLOAD THIS
FREE TOOL, SEE PAGE 339**

6 STEPS TO HANDLING TOUGH CONVERSATIONS

It's human nature to avoid conflict; we're wired in that way. I had a recent conversation with a leader in which he talked about how he avoided conflict, which cost him time, energy, and negatively impacted relationships with others. The principle I shared was this: Go toward the conflict. Our natural tendency is to move away from it and avoid it. It's only through what might feel like "rupture" that "repair" can happen. That's the upside of conflict handled well—improved relationships and trust.

Here are 6 steps to prepare:

IDENTIFY THE PROBLEM: 1

What do you need to communicate? Are business results not where they should be? Do staffing changes need to be made? Are there undesired behaviors that need to change?

_____

_____

_____

_____

_____

_____

IDENTIFY DESIRED OUTCOME: 2

What is your objective for the conversation? Are you trying to put business news in context for your employees? Do you need your team to understand changes that are underway? Do you need desired behaviors to become the norm among your staff?

_____

_____

_____

_____

TO DOWNLOAD THIS FREE TOOL, SEE PAGE 339

IDENTIFY YOUR AUDIENCE: 3

Who needs to hear this information?

_____

STRUCTURE YOUR KEY MESSAGES / CONVERSATION: 4

What do you want your audience(s) to think, feel and/or do?
- Consider how they might feel and receive the information you want to share.
- What concerns might they have and what perspective might they have?
- What are their needs and fears and do you share common concerns?
- How have you/they contributed to the problem and what would help it improve?

DELIVER YOUR MESSAGE: 5

Select the right time and place to have a conversation with privacy and without distraction. Encourage dialogue so you can get real-time insight on how employees are receiving the information and if they understand what you are saying.

FOLLOW UP: 6

Be sure to make yourself available to answer questions—in front of a group as well as privately. Ask what's on their minds and listen with empathy to people's concerns. Confirm next steps or expectations and timeline for completion.

A LEADERSHIP
~~ATTITUDE~~ (ALTITUDE)

Tough conversations are perfect times to set a positive example as a leader. This includes understanding and managing your own assumptions and emotions, especially when dealing with sensitive topics. Assumptions can get in the way of productive dialogue, so keep an open mind and don't assume you understand employees' intentions or attitudes without specifically asking. Also think about your own needs and fears and how they may contribute to your emotions.

For the best outcome, enter the conversation with a positive attitude and listen carefully to what is said verbally as well as through body language. However the conversation may progress, remain calm and view the discussion as objectively as possible, showing respect for employees' positions and the challenges they face.

To motivate with feedback, focus on the future

Even in times of change and challenge, sharing feedback with colleagues is a critical part of working together successfully. Yet many people I talk with feel they could do a better job giving feedback, whether by being more prompt or direct, or simply by ensuring a conversation happens. Giving feedback can feel uncomfortable, maybe even more so when it has to be delivered virtually. Personal discomfort aside, the truth is that most of us could be significantly more effective at work with regular input on what we're doing well and what could be better. Timely, frequent and specific feedback helps everyone improve. We can better recognize blind spots, know what to keep doing and when to change course, and benefit from building relationships with those who give us the gift of their advice.

How to give feedback that gets results

Research shows that for people to be motivated through feedback, the conversation must focus on the future. Recent studies published in *The Public Library of Science (PLOS) Journal* found that the willingness to change is greater when a feedback discussion focuses on future behavior, rather than on what happened in the past. By contrast, feedback conversations that focused on explaining past performance actually turned minor disagreements into major ones. "What mattered most for motivation to improve was how much the feedback conversation focused on generating new ideas for future success," explains study co-author Jackie Gnepp.

These results reinforce what we see in other aspects of leadership and change management. When people are involved in creating the path forward, they are more likely to be engaged and adopt changes to achieve a collective goal.

4 Fs OF FEEDBACK

When you're ready for a conversation, follow this proven methodology so people listen and act on your suggestions:

FRAME:

1

Ask permission. Then, share your motivation and intent.

First, ask whether now's a good time: "I have some feedback for you that I think will be helpful. Are you open to that right now?" If not, make an appointment. This ensures your employee or peer is in the right frame of mind for a productive conversation—if someone's having a bad day, it's better to postpone for another day. Then, set up the discussion with your motivation and intent in a way that establishes the benefit to the listener. This helps them not read into your actions with their own meaning.

FEEDBACK FOR THE FUTURE:

2

One behavior, then consequence.

Now it's time to discuss one specific and observable behavior and then the consequence. If there are a number of things you want to coach on, pick the most important to address first. One behavior at a time sets everyone up for the greatest chance of success. For example, "This behavior had this negative consequence (explain)" or "When you do (behavior), this is the (negative) result." Feedback should never be personal—avoid emotionally charged language or judgments and just state the facts as they are. Think about it this way—it's almost as if you had a video camera and were showing the individual a brief clip of a behavior of theirs and the consequence.

TO DOWNLOAD THIS FREE TOOL, SEE PAGE 339

FEELINGS:

3

"How do you feel about what I just said?"

Now, cultivate a two-way conversation by asking for a response in a very specific way. This demonstrates you genuinely care about the person's point of view and aren't just focused on delivering a corrective message. At this stage, you want to open up the possibility for both a feeling and thinking response. Don't just ask, "What do you think?" Chances are you'll get only a thinking response. A feeling response is much richer for the listener and often conveys more information. Ask directly, "How do you feel about what I just said?" Then, stop talking and listen. Listen actively and restate what you're hearing to show you understand their point of view.

If there's defensiveness move directly to discuss the alternative behavior you'd like to see in the future. Here, don't get caught in debating things. You shared the behavior and consequence, and now you need to ask for what you want to see instead in the future. Now's not the time for excuses or reasons; rather, it's time to take individual responsibility for one's actions.

FOLLOW UP:

4

How can I help you here?

Last, discuss specific next steps, including asking what you can do to help. This is another way to show you care. Also, take the opportunity to point out that feedback has become an important part of your leadership style, and that you're fostering an environment in which it will be common. Make sure your employees understand feedback is a two-way street, and that you expect them to feel comfortable sharing their thoughts with you in the spirit of continuous improvement. Of course, this means you must be open to their input and take appropriate action as well. Being timely and direct with feedback are essential for success.

CONNECTIVITY:

DESTROY EVERY "NORM" YOU THOUGHT YOU KNEW...

With so many of us working remotely, sometimes feeling connected 24/7, it may be hard to believe there are employees who are hard to reach with communication. Yet many organizations have important stakeholders with limited visibility to senior leaders, or even to their supervisors. These individuals may be constantly on the move away from their home base, on a production floor without phone or email access, or be part of a global organization that has team members literally in different worlds—across various continents, cultures, and time zones.

So, what can you do to engage with these hard-to-reach workers, while also managing those who would normally be in the office but are working remotely for the time being? Like any communication challenge, connecting with hard-to-reach employees (and all employees, for that matter) starts with thinking about your audience, then understanding how they want to get information.

WHAT IS IMPORTANT TO THEM?

WHAT BEST ATTRACTS THEIR ATTENTION?

WHAT INFORMATION DO THEY NEED TO DO THEIR JOBS?

HOW CAN YOU HELP CONNECT THE DOTS?

HERE'S HOW...

8 TIPS FOR CONNECTING WITH HARD-TO-REACH EMPLOYEES

1
COMMUNICATE PREDICTABLY

Be planful and strategic about keeping in touch with your team, especially in uncertain times when they may be worried and need encouragement. Set regular meeting times and encourage dialogue during meetings. Be sure team members know that out of sight doesn't mean out of mind and explain the best ways they can reach you if they need to. This helps them know that their input and questions are welcome and gives them a sense of when to expect feedback.

2
RESPOND QUICKLY

An afternoon can seem like an eternity to someone who is waiting for your input or response but can't see that you are busy or in an all-day meeting. Even a quick email or text is helpful to acknowledge receipt of their message and say when you can respond. Consider sharing your daily calendar with employees so they see when you're in meetings or out of the office. Do your best to answer questions when they are asked, and if you don't know the answer say so and follow up within 24 to 48 hours.

3

SHARE WHAT YOU KNOW, WHAT YOU DON'T KNOW, AND WHAT YOU'RE FIGURING OUT

Especially during times of change and uncertainty, employees need to hear from you more often, even when you don't have everything figured out. Chances are there's a lot that you know that would be helpful for your employees to hear. While you may be inclined to wait to communicate until you have more answers, more clarification, more details—resist the temptation to wait. It's best to share what you know and invite dialogue about what is on their minds.

4

APPRECIATE FREQUENTLY

The little things mean a lot to an employee who has few interactions with their manager or colleagues. Show appreciation for good work and recognize employees who deliver what you need or respond quickly, especially for those who aren't face-to-face with you and colleagues. Highlight the successes of hard-to-reach workers in team meetings, via company communications and the intranet.

5

SCHEDULE MORE PERSONAL TOUCHPOINTS

Hearing your voice and knowing that you took the time to reach out shows employees that they are valued. Use these opportunities to check in on how they are doing personally, what support they might need and how you can help. Take the opportunity to listen to their needs and gather input on what affects them.

6

TRAIN SUPERVISORS TO IMPROVE THEIR COMMUNICATION WITH PRODUCTION TEAMS/REMOTE WORKERS

Wherever they are, employees need to hear important messages repeatedly for them to sink in, and they want to hear from their managers. While employees rank managers as their most preferred information channel, many managers feel ill-equipped to communicate consistently, according to research from Gartner. Helping front-line leaders understand and practice effective communication can help their teams and the organization.

7

USE GROUP TEXT MESSAGING TO YOUR ADVANTAGE

Use group text messaging to deliver critical or urgent news to highly mobile workers. Incorporate this approach as a key channel and where possible link to articles/pages on the company intranet for more information.

8

PLAN REGULAR SHIFT MEETINGS

Hold regular shift meetings for all teams so supervisors can share company updates with employees. A planned cadence of connection points gives you regular and natural opportunities to share updates and open dialogue about various topics.

KEEP IN MIND

Employees need to know their voices are heard, whether they are on the move, with patients, on the shop floor, or working remotely with technology.

CHAPTER 8

USE THE RIGHT CHANNELS TO COMMUNICATE WITH IMPACT

WITH SO MUCH VOLATILITY IN OUR WORLD TODAY...

It is more important than ever to communicate effectively with employees. The right message, delivered at the right times and through the right channels, goes a long way toward building community and engagement. Particularly for teams that have suddenly become entirely remote, communication needs to accomplish a lot. It is one of the best and most powerful tools companies have in breaking down barriers and bringing people together. Communicators and leaders have a wide range of options for communication channels today, and the list of channels keeps growing. It wasn't long ago video conferences like Zoom and MS Teams were used far less than they are today. Still, having access to so many channels doesn't always mean your messages are received, heard, understood or acted upon. With more options to choose from, leaders need to ensure channels are selected strategically so employees aren't victims of information overload. Through this chapter, you'll get a quick overview of the key options and guidance on which channels may work best for your organization.

FACE-TO-FACE
MEETINGS

VIDEO
CONFERENCE
CALLS

TRADITIONAL
CONFERENCE
CALLS

TOWN
HALLS

PODCASTS

WRITTEN
COMMUNICATION

EMAIL

TEXT
MESSAGES

VOICEMAIL

BLOG

INTERNAL
SOCIAL MEDIA

INTRANET

EMPLOYEE
SURVEYS

INFOGRAPHICS

NOTICE
BOARDS

VIDEOS

YOUR
CEO

EMPLOYEE
AMBASSADORS

FRONT-LINE
MANAGERS

FACE TO FACE

MOST EFFECTIVE TO:

- Facilitate discussion for immediate action
- Discuss complex, confidential or sensitive topics
- Share high-level or detailed news/updates
- Ensure messages reach receivers
- Gather immediate feedback and input
- Encourage two-way dialogue

TIPS AND BEST PRACTICES:

- Insist on an agenda/meeting goals and stick to them
- Respect time allotments—if people know you start meetings on time, they'll rarely be late
- Use flip charts to capture the discussion and build on others' thoughts
- Ask questions to check for understanding and listen to what's being said (or not said)
- Before you adjourn, assign next steps

6 REASONS TO USE FACE-TO-FACE:

1. Demonstrate importance
2. Interpret thoughts and feelings
3. Enhance your credibility and trust
4. Build relationships
5. Gather feedback in real time
6. Demonstrate respect when addressing sensitive issues

WHILE IT TAKES MORE TIME TO HAVE A CONVERSATION, IT OFTEN *SAVES TIME* AND CONFUSION IN THE LONG-RUN.

VIDEO
CONFERENCE CALLS

MOST EFFECTIVE TO:

- Connect a team at times when they can't be together in person, while allowing for more intimacy than a phone call

- Enable screen sharing of valuable data in a highly visual and collaborative way

- Allow new team members to more quickly onboard, connecting faces with names

- Open up multiple communication queues, such as the body language and facial expressions of colleagues and clients

TIPS AND BEST PRACTICES:

- Recognize that virtual meetings are different from face-to-face, requiring a different approach, meaning more care is needed for employees to open up

- Plan ahead with important support materials. Send the agenda ahead of time. When appropriate, provide background materials too, such as pre-reads, charts and graphs

- Assign a facilitator to keep the meeting running smoothly, looking out for questions via chat functions

- Consider an icebreaker, inviting employees to share some introductions before launching into the business of the meeting

- Stick to firm timeframes and don't overload participants with too many objectives

- Ahead of the meeting, invite specific employees to contribute to portions of the meeting

9 STEPS TO COMBAT VIDEO CONFERENCE FATIGUE:

1. Ask yourself, do I really need a video conference for this conversation?

2. Ensure you're in "speaker view" so you're focused on the speaker and not distracted

3. Avoid multi-tasking

4. Take notes

5. Build in breaks to your day

6. Have shorter meetings

7. Turn your camera off

8. Mute yourself when you're not speaking

9. Switch meetings to phone calls when video isn't necessary

TRADITIONAL
CONFERENCE CALLS

MOST EFFECTIVE TO:

- Gather large groups together on a routine basis for alignment, to share news, to advance project plans, or to simply connect on the priorities for the week

- Allow for more informal and efficient check ins

- Give team members a break from too many video conference calls, particularly at the end of the day when teams may feel drained by video

TIPS AND BEST PRACTICES:

- Encourage more people to contribute by asking more specific questions of individual employees

- If one team member is dominating the conversation, shift the attention to a new topic or call on someone else to contribute

- Whenever possible, keep the calls short and to the point and adhere to strict timeframes

- Distribute summary notes with action items following the call for clarity and understanding

" THE ART OF COMMUNICATION IS THE LANGUAGE OF LEADERSHIP.

– James Humes, author and speechwriter

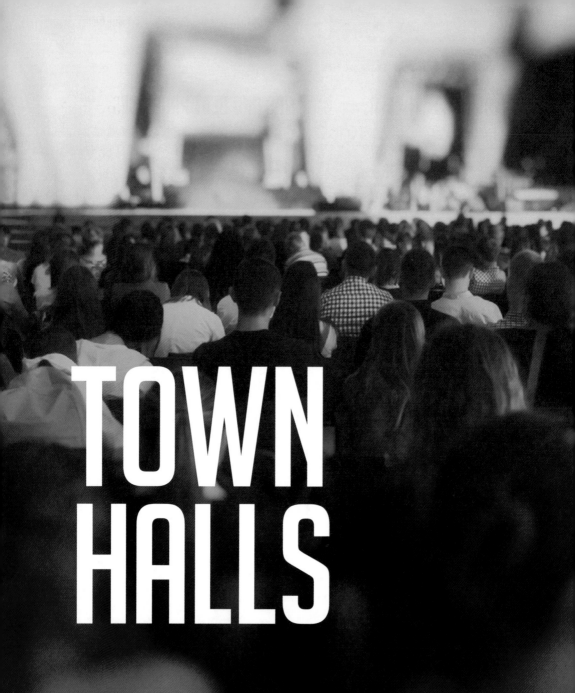

TOWN HALLS

MOST EFFECTIVE TO:

- Provide leaders an annual or quarterly opportunity to bring together the full team to discuss business developments and plans

- Recognize individual or team accomplishments

- Help the full team see the big picture for the business and upcoming milestones

- Motivate employees with an inspiring vision for the company's future

TIPS AND BEST PRACTICES:

- Don't just talk at employees; provide multiple opportunities for questions and conversation; during virtual town halls, this can be done with the chat function, Q&A moderator, etc.

- Avoid PowerPoint overload and dense slides that can turn off employees or bore them. Ensure the speaker is on video during virtual town halls

- Have a follow-up survey after the town hall to gain feedback and continuously improve

- Encourage leaders to host local meetings (virtual meetings work as needed) within two to three days after the enterprise-wide town hall so they can narrow in on key messages specific to their regions or functions

10 IDEAS FOR YOUR TOWN HALL:

1. Crowdsource questions
2. Use audience response technology
3. Hold a mini talk show
4. Use provocative questions
5. Feature a storytelling segment

6. Include case studies
7. Utilize gamification
8. Record your own "Carpool Karaoke"
9. Hold a real-time hashtag campaign
10. Incorporate an "Amazing Race" theme

PODCASTS

452 MILLION HOURS ARE SPENT LISTENING TO PODCASTS EACH WEEK IN THE U.S. ALONE[3]

 [3]Edison Research and Triton Digital, "The Infinite Dial 2020"

MOST EFFECTIVE TO:

- Share updates with people who are on the move (i.e., remote/traveling employees)
- Reach audiences that use the internet or portable devices frequently
- Elevate leadership visibility throughout the organization
- Tell stories or share a dialogue between key stakeholders on an important topic

TIPS AND BEST PRACTICES:

- Use informal language
- Keep your message short
- Use podcasts as a platform for employees to not only hear from leaders but from peers to drive engagement
- Build a following by releasing new podcasts regularly

HOW COMPANIES ARE USING PODCASTS IN NEW WAYS:

Companies such as Marriott also use podcasting as a way to reach potential job seekers. Recently, Marriott launched a podcast for job candidates called *The Wandernaut Show,* which highlights what differentiates Marriott from its competitors and shares the company's values through storytelling.

Johns Hopkins All Children's Hospital also recently launched its own *BlogTalkRadio,* which features 30-minute episodes and employee interviews that provide a "behind-the-scenes look at the people, places and work we do." The episodes feature doctors, nurses, leaders and other employees sharing their experiences in pediatric care.

WRITTEN
COMMUNICATION
(E.G., LETTER, MEMO, ETC.)

MOST EFFECTIVE TO:

- Share detailed information
- Provide a paper record of reference materials, policies, etc.
- Reach audiences with limited access to computers

TIPS AND BEST PRACTICES:

- Keep messages short and to the point
- Use when additional dialogue or conversation isn't necessary
- Use headlines and subheads/bullets to lay out messages in an easy-to-read format
- Make it visually attractive for an easier, more memorable read

5 MUST DO STEPS TO PLAN ANY COMMUNICATION:
(SEE "TAKE 5" ON PAGE 187)

1. **OUTCOME** *(what)* — The business outcome you seek

2. **AUDIENCE** *(who)* — Your audience, where they are coming from, and what you want them to think, feel and do

3. **MESSAGES** *(what are you trying to convey? why?)* — Given the audiences' mindset, list the 2-3 main messages to move them to action

4. **TACTICS** *(how and when)* — The most effective means of reaching your audience

5. **MEASUREMENT** *(listen for understanding and commitment)* — How you'll know when you're successful

EMAIL

MOST EFFECTIVE TO:

- Provide directional, important and timely information
- Share detailed information and data
- Direct the receiver to an online source for more information
- Provide brief status updates

TIPS AND BEST PRACTICES:

- Make the subject line relevant and meaningful
- Keep messages focused, easy to read and brief
- Don't put anything in an email you wouldn't want publicly broadcast
- Indicate if you need a response (what and when)
- If it takes more than two to three emails to bring closure to a topic, make it a voice-to-voice conversation (it's probably too complex for an email)

DO USE EMAIL TO:

- Provide one or multiple audiences with a brief status update in the body of a message
- Deliver a longer message or information as an attachment to your intended recipients
- Give timely information consistently to a group of recipients
- Prompt the recipient to view web-based content or other content that's attached

DON'T USE EMAIL:

- To give bad or negative news
- To give complex or lengthy information or instructions
- When the recipient deserves an opportunity to give immediate feedback or respond
- When there might be nuance or context that can't be understood by written words; to express feelings
- After multiple back-and-forths, pick up the phone

TEXT
MESSAGES

MOST EFFECTIVE TO:

- Notify employees about security issues
- Provide weather and/or travel alerts
- Send meeting and event reminders

TIPS AND BEST PRACTICES:

- Keep messages short and to the point
- Establish guidelines to prevent text message overkill
- Give employees an opportunity to "opt in" or "opt out"
- Know if there are certain times your company policy allows you to text

Did you know that

~83 BILLION

text and mobile messaging app messages are sent every day worldwide[4]

WOW!!! 😀

[4]Combined data from Teodora Dobrilova, "TechJury," 2020 & Statistica, "Mobile Messenger Apps - Statistics & Facts," 2019

VOICEMAIL

MOST EFFECTIVE TO:

- Communicate urgent, brief messages
- Request immediate response
- Ask simple questions that have quick responses
- Reach people when a meeting isn't possible
- Communicate with team members who are traveling

TIPS AND BEST PRACTICES:

- If working remotely, set your message to include your cell phone and/or home phone number so clients and colleagues can easily reach you
- Use if additional dialogue or conversation isn't necessary
- Avoid leaving a message about numerous topics
- Jot down what you're going to say before you say it; keep in mind the outcome you seek
- Begin with your main point. Leave your call-back phone number
- Indicate if you need a response (what and when)
- Keep messages short and to the point; don't ramble

COMMUNICATION WORKS FOR THOSE WHO WORK AT IT.

— John Powell, film composer

MOST EFFECTIVE TO:

- Create dialogue between employees and their leadership
- Demonstrate engagement from a leader(s) in a positive way, and hear their perspective on important topics
- Reach audiences that already use the internet frequently
- Share stories and inspire readers

TIPS AND BEST PRACTICES:

- Be authentic; blogs require a different tone and point of view than other vehicles
- Keep messages informative, timely and simple
- Use photos/visuals, section headers and bullet points when possible to visually break up the content and make it easy to read
- Don't just post messages—reply to others' comments to create dialogue and an exchange of information
- Appoint someone to moderate the discussion in comments
- Develop and share guidelines on using personal blogs to disclose company information

COMPANIES WHO WANT TO REMAIN COMPETITIVE AND SUCCESSFUL NEED TO ENSURE THEY INVOLVE, MOTIVATE AND INSPIRE COLLEAGUES.

— Viktoria Tegard, Head of Internal Communications, Virgin Atlantic Airways

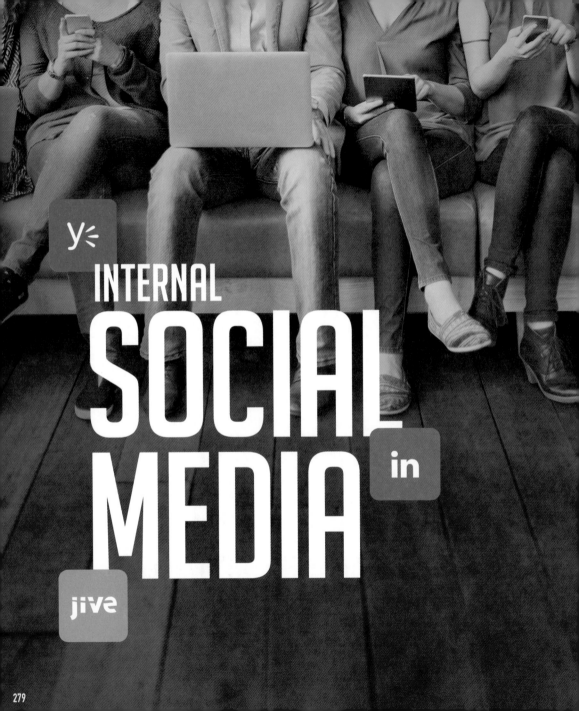

INTERNAL

SOCIAL

MEDIA

MOST EFFECTIVE TO:

- Establish open dialogue with employees
- Solicit feedback, which can be done with a formal poll or through the comments section
- Generate engagement among employees
- Integrate and share content from different platforms

TIPS AND BEST PRACTICES:

- Have a committed team of ambassadors to participate on internal social media and act as the face of the company
- Engage users with interactive content and by integrating popular social platforms (when appropriate)
- Set up social groups so teams can collaborate on projects in real time

INTERNAL SOCIAL MEDIA COULD INCLUDE:

- Company blogs
- Intranet articles that enable commenting, sharing or liking
- Team sites for collaboration and idea exchange
- Social platforms like Yammer, Workplace, Chatter or Jive
- Company-curated (member only) LinkedIn networks
- Behind-the-firewall video channels
- Other opt-in conversation and collaboration sites (now commonly built into intranet platforms like SharePoint)

INTRANET

MOST EFFECTIVE TO:

- Share successes, wins and best practices with large audiences (e.g. a department, a location or all employees)

- Provide access to applications, tools and data

- Share photos or videos that may be too large for email distribution

- Encourage collaboration through blogs and other social media tools

- Serve as a go-to hub for essential information related to employee health and safety, company policies, etc.

TIPS AND BEST PRACTICES:

- It should serve as a tool to help employees do their job better/faster

- Ensure the site is easy to use and navigate

- Keep content simple and up-to-date for credibility

- Make it interactive (e.g. polls, feedback channels, leader blogs, front-line employee blogs)

- Include a contact person for more information

- Send email reminders with a link to call out items that are new to draw attention

REMEMBER:
YOUR INTRANET SHOULD PROVIDE INFORMATION THAT HELPS MAKE YOUR EMPLOYEES' JOBS EASIER. IF IT DOESN'T, YOU RISK ADDING TO COMMUNICATIONS CLUTTER.

EMPLOYEE
SURVEYS

(E.G., ENGAGEMENT SURVEYS, EVENT-BASED FEEDBACK POLLS, FOCUS GROUPS, ETC.)

MOST EFFECTIVE TO:

- Gather employee feedback and insights
- Measure the effectiveness or impact of programs, initiatives, communications, etc.
- Show employees their opinion matters

TIPS AND BEST PRACTICES:

- Keep employees involved throughout the process; let them know what you heard and what will change as a result of their feedback
- Share survey results and communicate the areas of improvement on which you'll focus
- Take action on feedback

COMMON TYPES OF EMPLOYEE SURVEYS INCLUDE:

- Engagement surveys
- Surveys to know employees' understanding of a topic
- Employee communications need assessments
- Event-based feedback polls (such as after a town hall)
- Organizational assessment surveys
- Employee opinion polls
- Focus groups

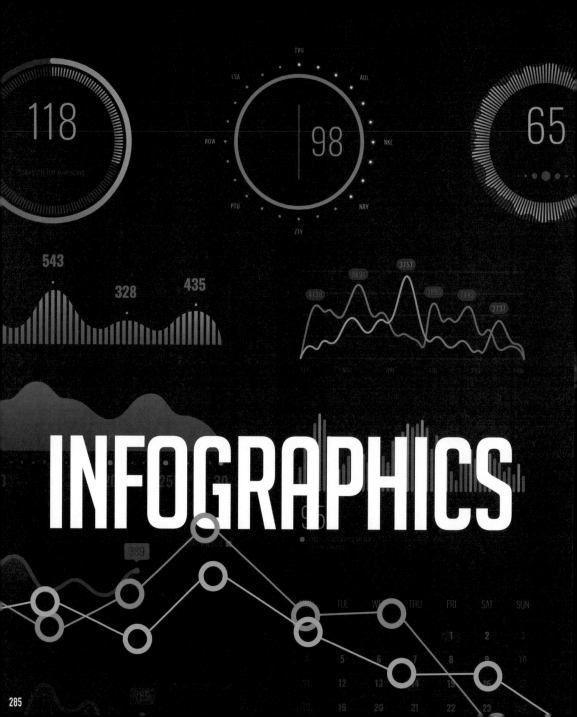

MOST EFFECTIVE TO:

- Quickly illustrate messages in a highly visual and easy-to-read format
- Share on social media to quickly articulate what a data set means
- Post on social media, the intranet and in newsletters or other publications

TIPS AND BEST PRACTICES:

- Ensure that you have a top-notch graphic storyteller who can make the message clear and easy to process quickly
- Use in place of a PowerPoint presentation when you need to get a message across with few words and powerful images

INFOGRAPHIC DOs:

- Keep it highly visual
- Have a succinct and compelling headline
- Show impact with fonts, colors and iconography
- Think about your audience and what's important to them
- Cite your sources

INFOGRAPHIC DON'Ts:

- Use text heavy phrases
- Cover too many topics
- Use jargon or unclear language
- Forget a clear call to action

NOTICE BOARDS

LEFT BRAIN VS. RIGHT BRAIN

The popular notions about "left brain" and "right brain" qualities are generalizations that are not well supported by evidence. Still, there are some important differences between these areas. The left brain contains regions involved in speech and language (Broca's area and Wernicke's area), and is also associated with mathematical calculation and fact retrieval, Holland said. The right brain plays a role in visual and auditory processing, spatial skills and artistic ability — more instinctive or creative things, Holland said — though those functions involve both hemispheres. "Everyone uses both halves all the time," he said.

The human brain is divided into two hemispheres, the left and right, connected by a bundle of nerve fibers called the corpus callosum. The hemispheres are strongly, though not entirely, symmetrical. The left brain controls all the muscles on the right-hand side of the body, and the right brain controls the left side. One hemisphere may be slightly dominant, as with left- or right-handedness.

Virtually, all stock photographers work alone or in small teams. They are all managed to scale. Several people have cloned themselves to produce more

Then there is collaboration. We can hire creatives for specific projects. Hire a famous photographer for a shoot. Contract a font foundry to create a set of fonts for us.

We are creating a system where very talented creatives can develop their own style and share everything. Some young talented kid comes along who can take better images than me. I'll open her images and add cherry to it to regain the number one spot. An amazing photographer takes a photo in New York and uploads it. By the end of the day, zero amazing retouchers have all edited in their own style and our best graphic designers have already added their graphic concepts to it. We keep hiring the most talented young people, we are doing this right now here in Thailand and soon we'll be able to start attracting the best young creatives from around the world. We don't need people with tons of experience, just brilliant artists straight out of uni or not.

MOST EFFECTIVE TO:

- Share information that does not require action and is not urgent (e.g. recognize individual employees or teams)

- Inspire employees by providing an easily visible display of progress being made

TIPS AND BEST PRACTICES:

- Establish guidelines for postings

- Ensure messages are easy to read

- Avoid clutter—remove outdated postings regularly

- Label different sections of the board to keep it organized by topic

- Use visuals and color to bring the notice board to life

WAYS YOU CAN USE NOTICE BOARDS TO CONNECT WITH ON-SITE EMPLOYEES:

- Label different sections of the board to keep it organized by topic (e.g. upcoming events, announcements, employee birthdays or workplace anniversaries, etc.)

- Post notices about HR policies and other pertinent information

- Recognize individual employees or teams for outstanding work or for their contributions to the community

- Introduce new team members with a brief Q&A and photos

- Use photos and colorful paper to bring the notice board to life and decorate it for holidays

- Rotate content weekly to ensure content doesn't get stale and employees look at it regularly

VIDEOS

MOST EFFECTIVE TO:

- Provide information and training on specific programs/initiatives
- Serve as an opportunity to "show and tell" about new products, new people, etc.
- Crowdsource content and engage through comments and/ or by linking to polls, resources pages, etc.

TIPS AND BEST PRACTICES:

- Appeal to visual and audio senses
- Video doesn't have to be highly produced to be effective; oftentimes small video shorts, with a clear message, resonate most with employees
- Make the videos fun and engaging
- Use subtitles so employees can read messages without audio as an option

75% OF EMPLOYEES *ARE MORE LIKELY* TO WATCH A VIDEO THAN TO READ DOCUMENTS, EMAILS OR WEB ARTICLES, ACCORDING TO FORRESTER

CUTTING EDGE

APPROACH TO CHANNELS

While the following are not always considered *"traditional channels,"* we think each of them are **critical** to getting any strategic message to resonate with employees.

YOUR

CEO

THE BACKSTORY:

There's no underestimating the growing importance of senior leader communications as a key communication source for ensuring any organization's success. Many recent studies have highlighted the critical importance of what CEOs say and the messages they impart. According to a recent McKinsey & Company study, a company transformation is 5.8 times more likely to be successful when CEOs communicate a compelling, high-level change story.

MOST EFFECTIVE TO:

- Ensure employees are hearing the message "from the top"
- Help employees see their leader as someone who truly cares about the strategy's success and wants to inspire and support his/her team to do their best work
- Facilitate a culture of listening as well as dialogue

TIPS AND BEST PRACTICES:

- Leaders need to understand just how much their communication matters to the success of any transformational effort
- Communicators should help leaders speak from the heart, and reveal more of who they are and what matters to them
- Avoid corporate speak/jargon in CEO communications (and all communications). Employees tune out quickly if the messages seem too formal or insincere

EMPLOYEE
AMBASSADORS

THE BACKSTORY:

Employee ambassadors are becoming an increasingly critical and effective channel of their own. A growing number of organizations recognize that ambassadors—when trained well—can serve as an informal but highly valued extension of any communications team. A recent study from The Conference Board, *The State of Employee Advocacy,* found most companies surveyed were "either already capitalizing on their workforce as spokespeople for the brand on social media, or planning to launch a program in the very near future."

MOST EFFECTIVE TO:

- Build a greater sense of unity among employees as "one team"
- Help to engage employees who want to play a bigger role in supporting the brand
- Push out highly effective and authentic voices in discussions of the company's strategy and value proposition

TIPS AND BEST PRACTICES:

- Know the risks and how you'll manage them. Before launching a program, make sure ambassadors understand the ground rules: No profanity, hate speech, bullying, inappropriate links, etc. Ambassadors also need to ensure all posts comply with FTC and SEC regulations.
- Involve employees in setting up the programs, train your ambassadors well, then trust them. No one wants to hear from employees who seem like blind supporters of the brand—genuine voices are key.

YOUR LINE
MANAGERS

THE BACKSTORY:

Increasingly, organizations are seeing the important role that line managers play in employee communications. While employees rank managers as their most preferred information channel, many managers feel ill-equipped to communicate consistently, according to research from Gartner. And more than a third (36%) are challenged in responding to negative reactions or difficult questions from their team members. In addition, 80% of change is driven at the manager level and 50% of managers are resistant themselves, according to Prosci data. When trained and prepared well, managers can be a major factor in any strategy's success.

MOST EFFECTIVE TO:

- Help front-line employees know exactly what they need to do to support a particular strategy or initiative
- Establish managers as personally standing behind the company's path forward

TIPS AND BEST PRACTICES:

- Take the time to ensure managers have the right training and resources to serve as a powerful communications vehicle
- Provide managers talking points and sample Q&As so they are most prepared to answer employee questions
- Give managers a template for generating regular discussions with their employees during shift huddles and other team meetings

CHAPTER 9

BE READY TO ANSWER
QUESTIONS

3 TIPS TO FACILITATE DIALOGUE AND UNDERSTANDING

Difficult questions. We all get 'em. Being prepared, and practicing three tried-and-true techniques can help you field with ease that challenging employee question (or the reporter who's looking for a compelling angle).

The first thing to know is it's best to answer the question. Directly. We've all heard non-answers and know what that feels like to be on the receiving end of some babble. Or someone who thinks "spin" can take the place of "truth." Your employees know the score, and your credibility (or lack of it) will be front and center in how you answer those tough questions.

1 PREPARE YOURSELF:

Be ready for the questions you're most likely going to get the most:

- What is on people's minds?
- What's the toughest questions you're likely to get— and how will you respond to them?

2 PRACTICE:

(OUT LOUD) to answer the questions that are likely to be the toughest:

- Think about the perspective your employees will bring to the discussion.
- Demonstrate empathy as you answer questions.
- Be respectfully authentic.
- Employ the 3 + 1 communications approach:
  - What we know...
  - What we don't know...
  - What we're working on finding out...

BRIDGE:

3

Bridging helps you get back on track if questions are starting to pull you down a path that isn't helpful, or distracts you from the key points you're trying to get across.

Key steps for bridging:

- Address the question being asked, but don't stop there.
- Use key words or phrases as a bridge to get back to a key point you want to make.

REMEMBER:

You can't just ignore a question you don't like. You need to address it, even if it is just to say that you don't have the answer at this time. You can bridge to a key message by using some phrases like these:

- "However…"
- "Something else that may be of interest…"
- "I can't speculate on that but what I can tell you is…"
- "What you should know is…"
- "The most important question we should all be asking is…"
- "Before we go too far down that path, let me add…"

EMPLOYEE QUESTION: "Is the date for returning to work going to be delayed beyond what the company originally announced?"

LEADER RESPONSE: "I don't know the answer to that right now. But what I can tell you is that our decisions on timing for getting people back in the office will be driven by our ability to have a safe working environment and guidance from state and local governments."

AND TO MAXIMIZE YOUR CREDIBILITY, HERE ARE 2 MORE TIPS

HOOK:

Increase curiosity about a topic

End your message with a statement that likely will prompt a follow-up question. Hooking can create dialogue focused on what you want to get across. And, it can also help you know whether people are actively listening.

Examples of hooking:

- "That's just one of the ways we're innovating to drive growth in the long-term…" (The natural follow-up is, "What's another way?")

- "Here's one result we're seeing right now…" (The follow-up is, "What are other results?")

FLAG:

Emphasize main points

Use flagging to emphasize or prioritize what
you consider to be the most important points.

Examples of flagging:

- "If you only remember one thing today…"
- "The most important point is…"
- "It boils down to this…"
- "The heart of the matter is…"
- "I can't underscore enough…"
- "Fact is…"

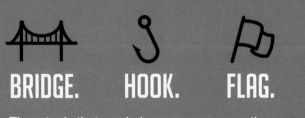

BRIDGE. HOOK. FLAG.

Three tools that can help you answer questions
with ease and ensure you're getting across what's
important to you, and your audience.

REPETITION
REPETITION
REPETITION
REPETITION
REPETITION
REPETITION
REPETITION

REPETITION
IS KEY

Don't just say something important once

Leaders who haven't realized the benefits of communication done well tend to think of it as a "check-off-the-box" activity. They'll think, "I sent an email. Therefore, I communicated." By doing so, they confuse getting the message out with actually creating shared meaning and understanding.

Recently, however, many leaders have seen the upsides to repeating important messages. When the pandemic hit, they quickly got crystal-clear on what needed to be said about workplace safety, COVID-19 protocols, work-from-home policies, among other critical topics, and they drove home the message. The result? In many cases, the workforce felt informed and trusted leadership to share vital information.

Follow up with materials to help your audience retain and process the message

Marketing research shows the average prospect needs to hear a message anywhere from three to 20 times before they take action. Employees don't need quite this same attention—their number is probably closer to three to five times—but it still takes a few reiterations for the message to sink in. Clearly, repetition is your friend. I often say, "If you're getting tired of delivering your message, then good for you. That means you're doing your job."

Engage key influencers and thought leaders along with supervisors throughout the organization

When employees hear the same messages from their supervisor (always their preferred source for job-related information), from the CEO, read it on the intranet, and hear it through the grapevine, they're more likely to believe it and, most important, act on it.

You should also remember that getting information out is just that—getting information out. Nothing more. To truly communicate, you need to know that the information was received and understood. In fact, doing a little and thinking you are done is one of the most common traps I see leaders fall into. The downside is a lack of information, skepticism, mistrust, confusion, or worse yet, inaction among those you are trying to reach. The opposite—especially in times of change and challenge—is to repeat what's important so you know employees understand it.

EMBRACE THE UNCOMFORTABLE TRUTHS

I grew up in Landsberg am Lech, a relatively small town in Bavaria, just outside Munich. Unfortunately, the town is well known for being the place where Hitler was imprisoned and later known as the "City of Youth" during Nazi rule. On the outskirts of the town were several concentration camps linked to the main site in Dachau. Growing up, I was removed from that era and experience, but I also wasn't exposed to much diversity outside of a summer or ski vacation to France and Austria. It was difficult to have perspective on topics of racism, intolerance, and discrimination. Yet as I entered college and started to spend more time abroad, I became more self-aware when people asked where I was from, which surfaced strong feelings of embarrassment and shame. While working in consulting early in my career,

I was even embarrassed to admit that I was German when colleagues detected an accent, especially when interacting with Jewish Americans. Never would I be comfortable to just say "I am proud to be German." These feelings made me appreciate even more my personal responsibility to stand up against racism to ensure this kind of past never repeats itself.

This journey has taught me that racial healing—and beginning to reverse the sins of the past—starts with honestly and publicly acknowledging a painful history, remedying as much as possible the wrongs committed, and moving forward from there. This challenge of continued personal growth and self-awareness can never end, and it requires me to consciously embrace an uncomfortable dialogue. It has also become part of who I am as a leader today. Now being a U.S. citizen, that perspective comes into play in a powerful way as we confront historical racism in corporate America and as a nation. I believe the first step is acknowledging that in fact there is a problem. As a leader at Hillrom, I'm encouraging more engagement, dialogue, and public conversation about systematic discrimination and violence. The conversations so far give me hope that we will make real progress and steps toward eradicating racism and intolerance in our public and private institutions and in the workplace.

Still, I am painfully aware of the amount of work that still needs to be done. I also see that our efforts need to reach a wide variety of historically disenfranchised groups that have felt left out of the conversation for years. At Hillrom, one way we're tackling that is by expanding our employee resource groups—for women, people of color, people with disabilities, LBGTQ, and a variety of others who request representation—to begin achieving a much stronger culture of diversity, inclusion and belonging. The voices coming out of those conversations are powerful and critical to shaping our future success. The journey we are on within corporations today needs urgency, coupled with continuous, genuine, and honest dialogue to bring about meaningful change. That's a new chapter in my history that I'm committed to for the long term, and this is a story I'm proud to write.

> **" THE VOICES COMING OUT OF THOSE CONVERSATIONS ARE POWERFUL AND CRITICAL TO SHAPING OUR FUTURE SUCCESS.**

Andreas Frank is President, Front Line Care at Hillrom, a global medical device provider. He also previously held leadership roles at Danaher Corporation and worked in the corporate finance and strategy practice at McKinsey & Company.

24

LEAN IN TO LISTEN AND LEARN

When we think about creating an inclusive culture, a mantra I learned from one of my mentors is to look for progress rather than perfection. I like to compare organizational change related to inclusion as a basket; it's necessary to have a series of changes interwoven into organizational systems. The changes need to involve strategy, talent, suppliers—essentially everything needs to be woven together. For leaders, the path to this kind of progress begins with true empathetic listening. That means that you start by leaning in to listen and learn from the person, not judge or problem solve.

> **" I LIKE TO COMPARE ORGANIZATIONAL CHANGE RELATED TO INCLUSION AS A BASKET; IT'S NECESSARY TO HAVE A SERIES OF CHANGES INTERWOVEN INTO ORGANIZATIONAL SYSTEMS.**

It's important, too, to enter a conversation about diversity and inclusion with a vulnerability and willingness to take on difficult, challenging discussions that will create new insights. It's important to recognize that we all have different experiences, and that even varies across the talented people on my team. It's important to recognize, respect and appreciate the significance of those differences. As leaders enter the conversation, they should inquire if the person is open to the conversation and how they are feeling. Then, leaders should ask: "Help me understand your experience" and they should be genuine about these kinds of queries. There also needs to be an acceptance on the part of the leader that what they hear may not be the same among and across a group of people; we all need to abandon the idea that "all,"—fill in the blank for gender, race, and ethnicity—do anything the same or have had a particular experience. These kinds of conversations need to be one-on-one and with a desire to discover the unique story of an individual.

Finally, it's important for leaders to commit to continuous communication: Revisit the initial conversations and set up new ones, all out of a desire to find the next right step, followed by another and another.

THAT'S
PROGRESS.

Sherri Dublin is Vice President of DE&I, Culture, Engagement & Communications for Ingredion. Sherri heads the Community of Expertise, responsible for the strategy, design and execution for DE&I, culture, engagement, and communication services. She works to enhance engagement and build an inclusive workplace culture that celebrates all diversity and cultivates innovation.

CHAPTER 10

BE RESPECTFULLY
AUTHENTIC

WHAT I HAVE LEARNED ON MY PERSONAL JOURNEY

I WANT TO INTRODUCE YOU TO WHAT I CALL *RESPECTFUL AUTHENTICITY,* WHICH AT ITS CORE IS ABOUT BEING TRUE TO YOURSELF AND ACTING IN WAYS THAT ARE CONSISTENT WITH YOUR VALUES.

Plus, there's a secret that authentic leaders know that most other leaders don't. The concept of authenticity has been around for a long time. I'm adding the word respectful to help distinguish it as a powerful tool in the workplace, one that eliminates many of the downsides that can come with simple authenticity. In this chapter, I'll address how to be more authentic, and will share some proven tools to help others get to know you better. I hope you don't mind that my thoughts here are a little more personal than you might typically read. However, I hope you'll see from my story that Respectful Authenticity is—in the end—hugely personal...

THE "SUPPOSED TO TRACK"

Growing up, I followed the "Supposed To Track"—get a part-time job at 16, earn good grades, graduate high school and college with honors, find the perfect corporate job, marry a gorgeous Jewish woman, have the cutest kids ever, and live happily ever after.

The feelings I allowed myself to have as a child, teenager and adult were solely happy ones; the rest of my feelings went into this deep, dark black hole never to be discovered or talked about. At 33, I had achieved what I was "Supposed To" and more, yet found myself in a therapist's office, almost to the week of the anniversary of my father's death, with a confusing message. Here's what I told her: "I'm married, have this house with a white picket fence and wonderful life in the suburbs, but have discovered that I'm gay and I'm going to have to leave my marriage and I'm really *happy* about all that."

"Really?" my therapist asked, wondering how I can be happy, knowing the traumatic events that were about to follow—coming out, and leaving my wife, home and life as I knew it. She saw right through the veneer of my polished, professional self.

It's then that I grabbed the pillow next to me and clenched it to my chest. **Hard.**

My therapist and I now laugh about the pillow that launched my journey of authenticity. In that moment, there was a significant disconnect between the words I was saying and my real feelings. I thought my therapist would mirror my happiness that day and that we would wrap everything up in a nice bow in six sessions. Instead, what she did was question my happiness and help me reflect on what a difficult thing I was about to do.

DISCOVERING ONESELF

As I reflect, there were a number of things holding me back from being myself. My sexuality was so repressed that I didn't feel that I was lying. I felt that I was authentically in love with my wife at the time I was married. It didn't feel like a lie or pretending. I had a ton of coping mechanisms to deal with the anxiety I felt.

MAKE NO MISTAKE. WHAT I'M SHARING WITH YOU IN THIS CHAPTER ISN'T A COMING OUT STORY; IT'S SO MUCH BIGGER THAN THAT.

It wasn't easy or fun coming to terms with being gay, although it became relatively black-and-white. The larger questions about who I was—the real me—and how to find contentment in life, and how to deal with life's stresses and worries, were more difficult. I know many of us might have thought about the larger question of, "Who am I?" I'd suggest if you haven't or haven't recently, it's worth thinking about. It's a big question, followed by many other related ones, and all of them are critically important influencers for how you lead.

Who are you today? What do you value? How do you ensure your life reflects what matters rather than just being carried by the waves of the day, or like me, feeling caught on a "Supposed To Track." Having answers to these important questions and understanding yourself at a deeper level will change your inner dialogue, how you spend your time, and most importantly, how you relate to others today. Plus, it gives you a view into the person you are yet to become. Part of therapy for me was also a unique experience of having a relationship with someone who I really didn't know, and where I couldn't tap any of my chameleon-like qualities. Much like a chameleon that has the ability to change colors, I had the ability to change my thoughts or feelings or attitudes in social situations to try and fit in. To be liked. To be accepted. Who doesn't want that?

One way to get to know someone, of course, is by asking them questions... and I tried that with my therapist, figuring that the more I know about her, the better I could relate to her. For every question I would ask her, she'd ask one in return...without answering my question: "If I did answer that, what would the answer mean to you?"

I was relentless in my asking questions of her, and she was relentless in her desire not to answer. All distractions from the real task at hand.

"THE DIFFICULT ROAD"

I quickly learned through that challenging period that I was going to have to go down what I now call "The Difficult Road"—this was very different from the "Supposed To Track" I was on—to get to where I wanted to be. I'm grateful now that I didn't question it. Deep inside, I knew this was a journey worth traveling. I was finally not terrified of being sucked into that black hole. If I did get sucked in, I knew I wasn't going to get lost in there forever; someone was going to pull me out. And it turned out that someone was me.

STARTING ON YOUR PATH

If you're thinking about how to differentiate yourself in the future, how to find your authentic voice and build trust with your teams, or help others do that, or lead a more fulfilled life, I have a few thoughts that I hope are helpful. Growing up, I watched way too much TV. My Saturday morning favorites were often cartoons or shows with heroes, and I was always rooting for the hero. I wanted desperately to have a superpower! Being the good guy or hero and making a difference was always important to me. Listening and responding to that impulse as an adult was a big part of my journey to become a more authentic person and leader.

I believe that starting on a personal path toward Respectful Authenticity is another way to make a difference for all leaders—for yourself and others, and it makes a real difference in improving your working relationships.

AUTHENTICITY MATTERS

As we continue to see high-profile business leadership and ethics scandals in the headlines, it's clear that trust in organizations today is eroding. On average, according to multiple studies, only one third of U.S. employees are engaged and less than half of that percentage are engaged globally. And there's no lack of stories about bad bosses today. Authentic people get better business results, have healthier work lives, and excel in real, meaningful relationships. They have high ethical and moral compasses because they know themselves and are outwardly focused. And they sleep better at night.

Employees feel more comfortable with an authentic leader. There are fewer question marks about what's on the leader's mind because employees know what to expect, and that's highly motivating. Employees not only like them, but want to follow them. In the end, authentic leaders create fundamentally different relationships with the people that they lead and their peers. Every person could benefit from being more authentic today. Every team could benefit from members who are more authentic. Every organization could benefit from employees and leaders who are true to themselves.

IMAGINE THE POSSIBILITIES FOR A MORE AUTHENTIC WORKPLACE...

With the significant focus on diversity, equity and inclusion inside workplaces today, Respectful Authenticity is more possible than ever before. There are tremendous positive outcomes from creating a work environment where anyone who's different is embraced and included for what they bring to the workplace... because everyone is being true to who they are.

If you see all this as possible, or aspire to help make the workplace better, or just want to be better yourself, I want to help you with this journey by coming at it from a place of self-knowledge and security in yourself.

AUTHENTICITY ISN'T A SKILL

What I know for sure from my experience, as well as from my research and consulting—which includes scores of interviews with senior leaders and practitioners—is that authenticity isn't a skill. It's a component of one's self that a person can accentuate or work on to become a better leader and lead a more fulfilling life, whether it's on the job, in your relationships, or at home.

No one really learns the skill of authenticity, but it clearly demonstrates itself through better communication. When you come at communication from an authentic place, communication becomes much easier and much more effective. I believe communication done well is a superpower because of all it can do for you, and not just because I wanted to have a superpower as a kid.

Here's the thing about communication—it's a skill that anyone can have, and it's easy to acquire. For a little bit of effort, the payoff can be significant. I know it might not always feel like communicating is easy; in fact, it might feel easier to NOT communicate. But not communicating IS communicating so you might as well get better at it.

WHAT RESPECTFUL AUTHENTICITY MEANS

Early in my career, I was fortunate to work with some incredibly inspiring leaders who brought out the best in me. I gravitated toward them because of how they made me feel. I trusted them because they were genuine, authentic, and because they demonstrated much more confidence in me than I had in myself. They stood for my potential, which was incredibly motivating for me as a 20-something professional, and only spurred me on to be even better.

When it was my chance to lead, I was determined to lead in a similarly authentic way. I tried to take the best strategies from each of them. After all, imitation is the greatest form of flattery. Still, I made my share of mistakes as a new leader, and then I realized an important lesson: Leading authentically isn't about being like someone else. Instead, it's about knowing yourself and being who you are.

Sure, you can "try on" strategies that work for others. Yet in the end, leading authentically is about finding what works best for you. And when you are genuine, you have "full power," which is what the Greek root of authentic—*authentikos*—truly means.

3 COMPONENTS TO RESPECTFUL AUTHENTICITY:

1. KNOW *Yourself*

2. BE YOUR *Best Self*

3. HAVE QUIET *Courage*

1. KNOW *Yourself*

KNOW YOURSELF IS THE FIRST COMPONENT

How do you do that? Here are a couple of ideas to consider; you choose what's best for you: ***Pay attention to what you already know about yourself.*** Maybe we don't always know ourselves totally, but we can stop and examine an experience we're having, and know whether it feels good or bad. And trust our gut feeling on it. As you have experiences, think, "Is This Me, or Not Me?" Get to know yourself as well as you can today…in this moment, and know that as time goes on, you will change and grow.

Make an inventory. Think about a half dozen instances where you were told or you felt you weren't authentic. Try and get an understanding of what got in the way. Then ask yourself, if you could have a do-over, what would you do differently? What learnings can you take forward to help you be more of who you are.

Get a better sense of your leadership style, and there are a myriad of ways to get feedback. Do a 360. Myers-Briggs. Read StrengthsFinder 2.0, or many of the other fine books that include leadership diagnostics. Use the results as an opportunity to hold a mirror up to yourself to see what you can learn further about yourself and how you lead.

Make a list of people you admire who are authentic. Write down what they do that leaves you with such a positive feeling. Try one of those behaviors for a week and ask yourself, "Is This Me, or Not Me?"

Have a "truth teller" or two around you.
Each of us has a best friend outside of work who tells us what we need to hear, even when it's tough love. We need the same at work. All of us have blind spots, and it's a truism that the higher you go in an organization, the greater the tendency is that people will tell you what they think you want to hear instead of what you need to hear. Truth tellers can help us know what we can't see ourselves.

IN THE END, THE MORE YOU KNOW YOURSELF, THE MORE EFFECTIVE YOU'LL BE.

2. BE YOUR
Best Self

THE SECOND COMPONENT IS TO BE YOUR BEST SELF AND ACT IN WAYS THAT ARE CONSISTENT WITH WHO YOU ARE

This is your own self-awareness as you relate to others. This means behaving in ways that are in sync with your values instead of simply trying to please others or get something from others. Do you recall how I described how I used to act as a chameleon and would change my thoughts or feelings based on how I thought others would react to me?

Today, I strive to be my authentic self regularly. What it looks like and how I act really doesn't change very much. What does change is how I feel on the inside. When I acted as a chameleon, I did it out of a desire for people to like me. I genuinely wanted people to like me. When I relate to others from an authentic place today, I do it with a sense that people will like me. I don't worry that they won't. They might not, and that's their choice—that's okay. I'm not consumed with the need for people to like me.

How do you know if you're being your best self?

Talking out loud can help you know whether what you're thinking about is in sync with your values. Just being able to listen to yourself day-to-day allows you to self-correct. You need to be able to say, "Wait a minute. I just heard what I said, and I'm changing my mind on that." Or, "That doesn't feel like me." Remember, "Is This Me, or Not Me?" You can listen to yourself on your own, or for more challenging topics or situations, enlist someone else to listen to you—not to make suggestions or give you advice, but to allow you to hear yourself and determine what's best for you. This is one of the many roles a great executive coach or therapist can play. This also can be a best friend, a colleague or spouse.

THE KEY IS SIMPLY THAT YOU HAVE THE OPPORTUNITY TO LISTEN TO YOURSELF.

3. HAVE QUIET *Courage*

AND FINALLY, THE THIRD COMPONENT: HAVE QUIET COURAGE AS YOU RELATE TO OTHERS

Authenticity is about this constant process of being truthful—first with yourself and then with others. To say the things that need to be said, and to do it in a kind and respectful way. Being authentic isn't about saying whatever you think or feel. That approach can be damaging either to you personally or to the company. Being authentic doesn't give you license to be an S.O.B. We all know people who've taken this kind of approach—the "This is me—like it or not!" attitude or "I'm mad and am entitled to yell at people." By contrast, Respectful Authenticity isn't about doing whatever you want and not caring about the people around you.

Remember the secret that I said authentic leaders know that other leaders don't know? The most successful authentic leaders share their truths with Quiet Courage, and with a sensitivity to others' needs. They understand that their work is not solely about them, but about building a powerful, effective team. Authentic leaders also flex their leadership style. They consider what the audience can understand, process and make use of. Giving someone information they have little way to process or understand can just create confusion and anxiety.

All this requires reflection on your part before you speak or act. In other words, you have to be planful and purposeful (you can't wing it), and that allows you to respond in a more grounded way.

WHEN YOU DO, YOU CAN TRUST YOURSELF MORE AND BE MORE CONFIDENT WHEN YOU KNOW YOU'VE THOUGHT THINGS THROUGH.

FROM A COMMUNICATION STANDPOINT, AUTHENTIC LEADERS UNDERSTAND THE AUDIENCE AND CONTEXT, AND THEN FLEX THEIR STYLE TO MEET THE NEEDS OF THEIR AUDIENCE

While this might sound like Communications 101, to be audience-focused is not common practice. One of the most common mistakes leaders make is to communicate from their perspective. We're all clear in our heads what we think. Moving someone to action isn't about what we think; it's about helping someone else think differently so they can then act.

If you're wondering about how you relate to others, one of best ways to know is to ask. Authentic leaders want to hear feedback to know how they're impacting others. It comes from a place of really wanting to know so they can shift what they're doing to better meet an employee's needs or to better motivate that employee. It's a different way to hold a mirror up in terms of understanding how you impact others by being interested and taking their feedback to heart.

I HOPE YOU CAN SEE WHY *QUIET COURAGE*, AS I CALL IT, ISN'T "RAMBO COURAGE" BUT AN INTERNAL KIND OF COURAGE THAT COMES FROM DEEP INSIDE.

WE RESPECTFULLY AUTHENTIC · CHAPTER 10

BE RESPECTFULLY AUTHENTIC · CHAPTER 10

WE ALL HAVE MORE COURAGE THAN WE REALIZE

My Mom passed away eight years ago. I knew the day would come, yet it was way too soon. She had been diagnosed with leukemia, and the worst kind. GG, as she was called, had two goals, and was uncharacteristically direct with her doctor the day she was diagnosed: "I have a grandchild coming and my grandson's wedding, and you're going to help me get there," she said, pointing at him. My Mom abhorred pointing.

I thought to myself, "That's what I call determination." I would come to find out how determined she was. I always thought I was a courageous person. Someday, I hope to have half the courage she had. The Yiddish word is "Chutzpah," which means guts; gall. At one point during her chemotherapy, she said to me, "I've realized that I have more courage than I ever thought I had."

I think that's true for all of us. We have more courage than we might think. It's often the moments that challenge us most, where we can learn the most. We don't need to wait for some terrible event to internalize this realization and to bring forward the Quiet Courage we have and the vulnerability that helps us connect with others.

3 Things

TO TAKE WITH YOU ON YOUR JOURNEY

If you're up for the journey to Respectful Authenticity—and I hope you are—here's what's important to have with you at all times:

First,
YOUR CURIOSITY

I asked a lot of questions as a kid. In fact, it got me in huge trouble with adults. I was the precocious kid who wanted to know how things worked, and why the world was as it was. To be authentic, you need to be curious about yourself, about others, and about the world.

You can't be authentic without the ability to reflect and be self-aware. You have to be curious despite any of the other feelings you might be experiencing—whether it's concern or worry, or other uncomfortable feelings like fear and shame. If you can be curious, you can look at anything. You can say, "Hmmm...Wow that's interesting...Is there something worth exploring here? Is there something I can learn about myself or others?" To get ahead in business, you need to continually be learning and growing.

Plus, curiosity will make you a better listener. Each of us, and the leaders we work with, can improve their listening. The better you listen to others, the better they will listen to you. The better they listen to you, the better your relationships will be, including your most important relationship—the one you have with yourself.

Second,
EMBRACE WHO YOU ARE

After all, it's our imperfections that create connections with others. People say all the time to "let it go"— the phrase that made the movie, "Frozen," so popular. You can never let go what you haven't embraced. You have to say, "This is mine. I can hold it. I can own it. Now, I can let it go." Once you really accept it, saying, "Yes, this is me. It's not my favorite part of me and now I can begin the process of letting it go and setting it aside because it doesn't really control me."

Last,
FOCUS ON WHAT YOU CAN CONTROL

Think about all you have control over, and focus on that. Not the economy. Not your competitors. Not what colleagues are gossiping about. But what's in your control. You can expend all your energy on what you can't control, or take that energy and passion and use it for good—to focus on meaningful change. One of the things you can control is how you communicate. Being planful and purposeful can significantly increase your chances of being heard and achieving your goals.

AS YOU THINK ABOUT AUTHENTICITY, REMEMBER THAT YOU HAVE POWER

And you have choices. You are stronger than you even know. Earlier on in this book we talked about how much courage you have inside you. And you always have more choices than you might think. No matter what you seek, you can create next steps for yourself rather than following someone else's pre-determined path. A big part of my journey was learning about myself— about how to not get trapped, and that I always have choices, even when I'm not at first able to see them. The choices are there; I now know I just have to look harder.

As you move forward on this journey, know that you aren't going to fail; you will succeed and continue to learn about yourself. If you find yourself stressed, or feel stuck, just listen to yourself, to your gut, take a step back and try to see the forest through the trees. When you're approaching a mountain and are miles out, it seems really small. When you get to the bottom of the mountain and look up, you realize it's huge. When life gets too big, back up a little bit. Sometimes when you're too close to something, it can feel overwhelming. You feel incapacitated and can't take the first step. Yet it's so helpful to just put your nose down and start. A CEO I used to work with often would say, "Jump in; the water's fine!"

THE VALUE OF FEELING AUTHENTIC

I now know the value of feeling authentic. This is the other side of the anxiety I felt. I had all sorts of ways to fend off and cover up my anxiety. The process of looking at yourself can be very difficult in the beginning. But the value at the other end can be so worth the process. Today, I know there is no black hole that I'm going to slip and fall into. There is a great level of security. It's this level of security in oneself, and the whole spectrum of feelings that go with it, that I wish for you. To become un-frozen from what gets in the way…enjoy the pleasure of being even more of who you are…and relish in your Quiet Courage to be truthful, curious, embrace who you are, and focus on what you can control.

I shared with you what the "Supposed To Track" looked like for me, but I'd like to fast forward to now. If you're not sold on authenticity, I want to share three more very personal reasons to embrace the journey and where "The Difficult Road" might lead you.

This is my husband Steve and my daughter, Avi. She's 11, going on 14 or 16, depending on the day. She's our Old Soul. Avi loves Anime, Cosplay, "Stranger Things," and has my perfectionist tendencies, which we're working on.

And to the left is her little sister, Noa. She's eight. She's kind and has a wicked sense of humor. A good moment of silence, which can be rare in our family sometimes, can lead to a one-liner that's remembered for years. She's obsessed with cats, although our busy home is a pet-free zone, except for a tank full of fish, which I agreed to after a few too many Margaritas. Noa also loves Anime, which I think is also a nod to how much she looks up to her sister, and how close they've become after so much quality time together.

NOA WAS THE GRANDCHILD MY MOM WAS WAITING FOR

And thank goodness she came early. Two weeks early. The minute we could leave the hospital we whisked her up to Milwaukee to meet my Mom.

And I'll always remember the moment I took Noa from my arms and put her in my Mom's. And for that one moment, everything was perfect in the world!

My Mom held Noa five times before she decided to stop treatment, and died.

My Journey

started with a pillow and took me down "The Difficult Road," and lots in between, and brought me here, to this moment, and will take me forward.

Where are you on your journey?

The time is now. The choice is yours.

What will your next step be?

CLOSING

THOUGHT

As we've learned during this challenging time, the ability to adapt and grow through change is going to be a key differentiator for leader success *long* into the future. Along your journey, if you're ever unsure of where to turn, ask yourself: "What would the best version of myself do?" In this unforgettable year—*A Year That Changed Everything*—I've seen countless leaders do just that, embracing change as a reality and an opportunity to learn and grow.

AND ABOVE ALL ELSE
HAVE THE COURAGE
TO LEAD WITH

HEART
F1RST

HEART F1RST

PROVEN LEADER TOOLS

As a special value-add to help you lead and communicate even better going forward, *Heart First* readers have exclusive access to The Grossman Group's most sought-after and often-used leader tools.

To gain access, visit the page below and use special code HFL21

WWW.YOURTHOUGHTPARTNER.COM/HEART-FIRST-RESOURCES

THE GROSSMAN GROUP

About | Consulting Services | Management Tools | Leadership Speaker | Executive Coach | Free Downloads | Books | Blog | Contact | COVID-19 Resources

HEART F1RST

THE GROSSMAN GROUP'S PROVEN LEADER TOOLS

As a special add-on to help you lead and communicate even better in the future, *Heart First* readers have exclusive access to The Grossman Group's most sought-after and often-used leader tools. These are the same tools that have been licensed by dozens of Fortune 500 organizations, and are proven to work by saving you time and increasing your effectiveness.

Fill out the form below (and enter the special code on the next page) to access the tools today!

Get access to the Proven Leader Tools today!

First Name*

Last Name*

Job Title*

Company Name*

Email*

Phone Number

GET THE TOOLS

340

DAVID GROSSMAN

ABC, APR, Fellow PRSA

DAVID HELPS LEADERS DRIVE PRODUCTIVITY AND GET THE RESULTS THEY WANT THROUGH AUTHENTIC AND COURAGEOUS LEADERSHIP AND COMMUNICATION.

David is both a teacher and student of effective leadership and communication. He is one of America's foremost authorities on communication and leadership inside organizations, and a sought-after advisor to Fortune 500 leaders. By acting as an advocate for employees and as a **thought**partner™ to senior management, David helps organizations unleash the power of communication to engage employees and drive performance.

David is Founder and CEO of The Grossman Group, an award-winning Chicago-based communications consultancy focused on organizational consulting, strategic leadership development and internal communications. Clients include Abbott, Amsted, Form Technologies, Hillrom, KeHE, Lockheed Martin, Novartis, SC Johnson, Southern New Hampshire University and Tecomet, among others.

David is often quoted in media, providing expert commentary and analysis on how leaders and companies can build trust and keep employees engaged through crisis and change, communicating with remote teams and more. He's been featured on "NBC Nightly News," *CBS MoneyWatch,* in *Forbes,* the *Chicago Tribune, World Economic Forum* and the *LA Times.*

Leaders, communication professionals, and educators applaud David's books— *You Can't **NOT** Communicate: Proven Communication Solutions That Power the Fortune 100,* and its follow up, *You Can't **NOT** Communicate **2*** and *No Cape Needed*—which continue to receive accolades and praise for reminding leaders— everywhere and at all levels—on the value of getting leadership and communication right. David's leader**communicator**™ blog has been ranked the number one blog on communications by Feedspot five years in a row.

Twice named *PR Week's* "Boutique Agency of the Year" and *The Holmes Report's* "Employee Communication Agency of the Year," The Grossman Group's work has won all the "Oscars" of communication. The Grossman Group is a certified diversity supplier. Prior to founding The Grossman Group in 2000, David was director of communications for McDonald's.

BRING THE INSIGHTS FROM *HEART FIRST* TO LIFE WITH YOUR TEAM

THE GROSSMAN GROUP

8 WAYS TO LEAD WITH HEART
IN TIMES OF UNCERTAINTY AND CHANGE

Invite David to present a powerful *Leading with Heart* training to your organization.

David Grossman is a sought-after speaker, consultant and executive coach, acclaimed for his highly engaging, interactive, and effective programs. He's known for a thoughtful, personal, and pragmatic approach that leverages communication as one of the ultimate business tools. From Fortune 500 companies and start ups to professional associations and universities, David's proven leadership communication programs benefit leaders at all levels and help them connect the dots between communication and business results.

Book David for a *Leading with Heart* training program and learn how to:
- Show your human side and listen with empathy and caring
- Frame the context for the current situation and make it relevant for your team
- Be ready to answer questions, especially the tough ones
- And much more!

David also addresses:
- How Top Leaders Differentiate Themselves
- How Communication Directly Influences the Bottom Line
- Communication in a New or Changing Workplace
- Leadership Practices that Create Productive Workplaces

To invite David to speak to your organization or team, or for more information, please visit:
www.YourThoughtPartner.com/Speaking-and-Events
or contact us directly at **312.829.3252** or
Results@YourThoughtPartner.com.

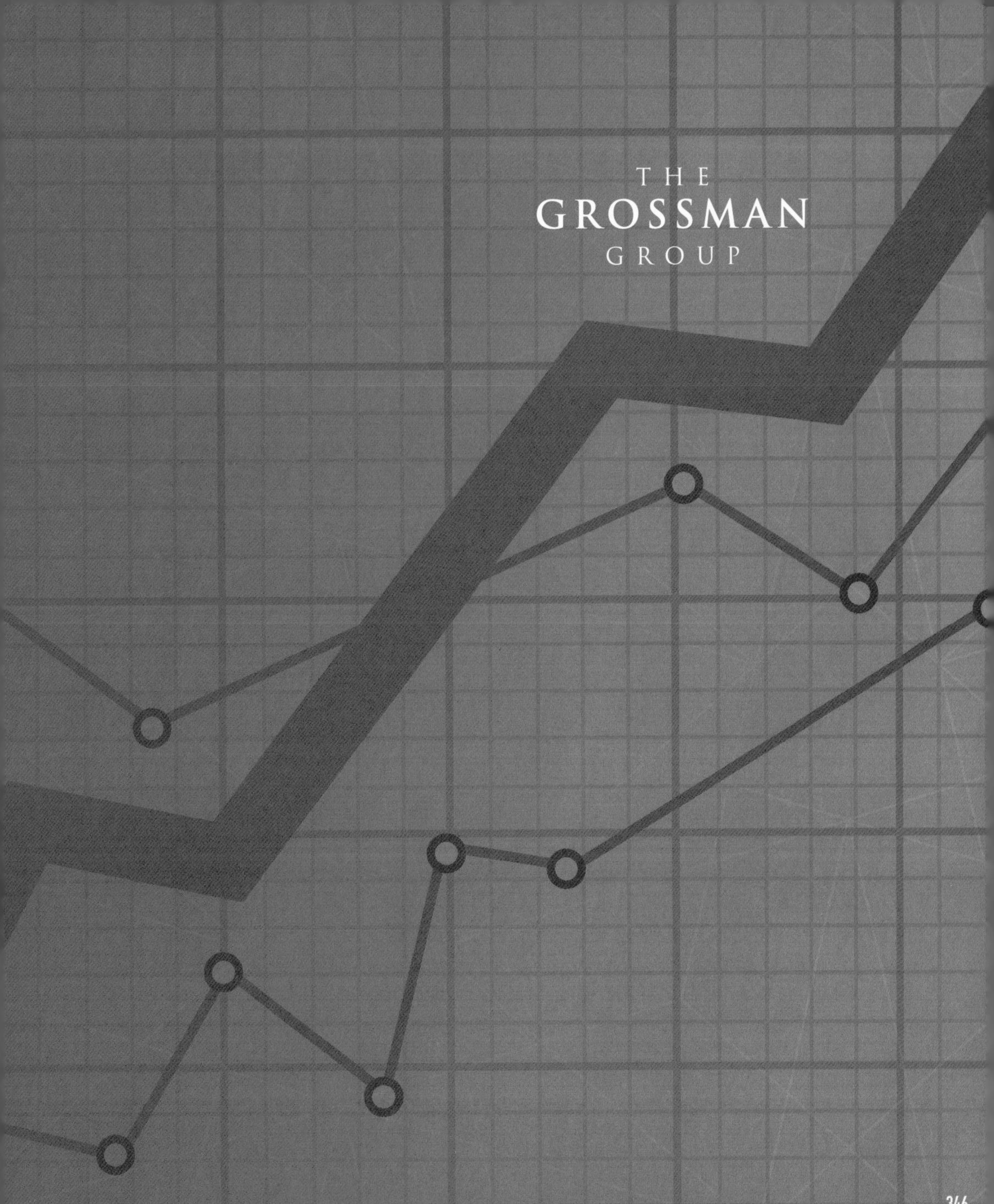
THE
GROSSMAN
GROUP

GET DAVID'S BOOKS

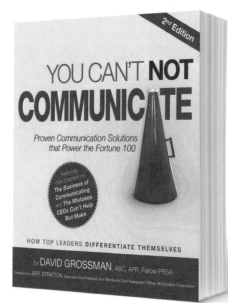

A must-read highlighting the importance of communication in bridging the organization's strategies and goals with an individual's performance.

- Norm Wesley, Former Chairman and CEO, Fortune Brands

Practical, wise, smartly designed— an example of what it recommends to its readers.

- Jon Iwata, Senior Vice President, Marketing and Communications, IBM Corporation

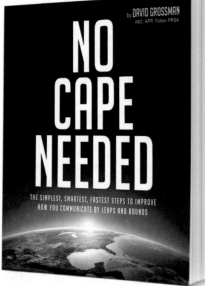
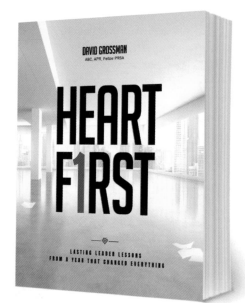

LET'S CONNECT

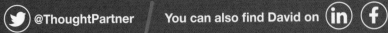 @ThoughtPartner / You can also find David on

VISIT OUR WEBSITE

Learn more about The Grossman Group and its proven approach to strategic leadership and internal communication. **YourThoughtPartner.com.**

CONTACT THE GROSSMAN GROUP

Are you looking to elevate your team or organization's performance? Call or email us today and we'd be happy to talk about how we can leverage our experience on your behalf. Call **312.829.3252** or email: **Results@YourThoughtPartner.com.**

SUBSCRIBE TO eTHOUGHTSTARTERS

For quick, simple tips to help build better leadercommunicators, subscribe to David's eThoughtStarters newsletter. **YourThoughtPartner.com/eThought-Starters.**

GET QUANTITY DISCOUNTS

Books are available at quantity discounts on orders of 50 copies or more. Please call **312.829.3252** or email at **Office@YourThoughtPartner.com.**

BOOK DAVID TO SPEAK AT YOUR EVENT

To help your leaders be better communicators, invite David to speak to groups large and small. **YourThoughtPartner.com/Speaking-and-Events.**

READ MORE ON THE BLOG

Thousands of readers receive regular communication tools and best practices from David. You can do so too, by subscribing to his award-winning leader**communicator**™ blog. **YourThoughtPartner.com/Blog.**

HEART F1RST

LASTING LEADER LESSONS
FROM A YEAR THAT CHANGED EVERYTHING

by **DAVID GROSSMAN** ABC, APR, Fellow PRSA